Number 143
Fall 2014

New Directions for Evaluation

Paul R. Brandon
Editor-in-Chief

Building a New Generation of Culturally Responsive Evaluators Through AEA's Graduate Education Diversity Internship Program

Prisca M. Collins
Rodney Hopson
Editors

BUILDING A NEW GENERATION OF CULTURALLY RESPONSIVE EVALUATORS
THROUGH AEA'S GRADUATE EDUCATION DIVERSITY INTERNSHIP PROGRAM
Prisca M. Collins, Rodney Hopson (eds.)
New Directions for Evaluation, no. 143
Paul R. Brandon, Editor-in-Chief

Microfilm copies of issues and articles are available in 16mm and 35mm, as well as microfiche in 105mm, through University Microfilms Inc., 300 North Zeeb Road, Ann Arbor, MI 48106-1346.

New Directions for Evaluation is indexed in Education Research Complete (EBSCO Publishing), ERIC: Education Resources Information Center (CSC), Higher Education Abstracts (Claremont Graduate University), SCOPUS (Elsevier), Social Services Abstracts (ProQuest), Sociological Abstracts (ProQuest), and Worldwide Political Science Abstracts (ProQuest).

NEW DIRECTIONS FOR EVALUATION (ISSN 1097-6736, electronic ISSN 1534-875X) is part of The Jossey-Bass Education Series and is published quarterly by Wiley Subscription Services, Inc., A Wiley Company, at Jossey-Bass, One Montgomery Street, Suite 1200, San Francisco, CA 94104-4594.

SUBSCRIPTIONS for individuals cost $89 for U.S./Canada/Mexico; $113 international. For institutions, $334 U.S.; $374 Canada/Mexico; $408 international. Electronic only: $89 for individuals all regions; $334 for institutions all regions. Print and electronic: $98 for individuals in the U.S., Canada, and Mexico; $122 for individuals for the rest of the world; $387 for institutions in the U.S.; $427 for institutions in Canada and Mexico; $461 for institutions for the rest of the world.

EDITORIAL CORRESPONDENCE should be addressed to the Editor-in-Chief, Paul R. Brandon, University of Hawai'i at Mānoa, 1776 University Avenue, Castle Memorial Hall Rm 118, Honolulu, HI 96822-2463.

www.josseybass.com

Editorial Policy and Procedures

New Directions for Evaluation, a quarterly sourcebook, is an official publication of the American Evaluation Association. The journal publishes works on all aspects of evaluation, with an emphasis on presenting timely and thoughtful reflections on leading-edge issues of evaluation theory, practice, methods, the profession, and the organizational, cultural, and societal context within which evaluation occurs. Each issue of the journal is devoted to a single topic, with contributions solicited, organized, reviewed, and edited ·by one or more guest editors.

The editor-in-chief is seeking proposals for journal issues from around the globe about topics new to the journal (although topics discussed in the past can be revisited). A diversity of perspectives and creative bridges between evaluation and other disciplines, as well as chapters reporting original empirical research on evaluation, are encouraged. A wide range of topics and substantive domains is appropriate for publication, including evaluative endeavors other than program evaluation; however, the proposed topic must be of interest to a broad evaluation audience. For examples of the types of topics that have been successfully proposed, go to http://www.josseybass.com/WileyCDA/Section/id-155510.html.

Journal issues may take any of several forms. Typically they are presented as a series of related chapters, but they might also be presented as a debate; an account, with critique and commentary, of an exemplary evaluation; a feature-length article followed by brief critical commentaries; or perhaps another form proposed by guest editors.

Submitted proposals must follow the format found via the Association's website at http://www.eval.org/Publications/NDE.asp. Proposals are sent to members of the journal's Editorial Advisory Board and to relevant substantive experts for single-blind peer review. The process may result in acceptance, a recommendation to revise and resubmit, or rejection. The journal does not consider or publish unsolicited single manuscripts.

Before submitting proposals, all parties are asked to contact the editor-in-chief, who is committed to working constructively with potential guest editors to help them develop acceptable proposals. For additional information about the journal, see the "Statement of the Editor-in-Chief" in the Spring 2013 issue (No. 137).

Paul R. Brandon, Editor-in-Chief
University of Hawai'i at Mānoa
College of Education
1776 University Avenue
Castle Memorial Hall, Rm. 118
Honolulu, HI 968222463
e-mail: nde@eval.org

CONTENTS

EDITORS' NOTES

This issue of *New Directions for Evaluation* (NDE) coincides with the 10th anniversary of the American Evaluation Association's (AEA's) Graduate Education Diversity Internship program (hereinafter referred to as GEDI). It also comes at an important juncture in the history of the field and the AEA, as the membership of AEA recently reviewed and passed a Public Statement on Cultural Competence in Evaluation (AEA, 2011). Additionally, the field has continued to recognize a swell of interest in professional development, training, and conference presentations about the role of culture and diversity in evaluation. It is therefore a timely moment to stop and reflect on the major diversity training programs implemented by the association.

The increased awareness of and sensitivity to issues of diversity within the evaluation field has resulted in an increased promotion of and need for cultural competence in our work (AEA, 2011; SenGupta et al., 2004). Over the years, the AEA's response to the need for increased cultural competence involved a rearticulation of theory, policy, methodology, practice, and commitment to strategic diversification of the evaluation profession. This was accomplished through AEA's support of a number of initiatives that promoted diversity and cultural responsiveness.

The GEDI program was conceived out of the efforts of the AEA Building Diversity Initiative (BDI) that was launched in 1999. Prior to the launching of the BDI, however, the AEA had initiated multiple diversity efforts that included development of a Topical Interest Group (TIG) on Multi-Ethnic Issues in Evaluation (formerly Minority Issues in Evaluation), creation of diversity-focused themes for its annual meeting (e.g., *Evaluation and Social Justice* by President Karen E. Kirkhart in 1994 [Kirkhart, 1995]; and *Transforming Society through Evaluation* by President Donna Mertens in 1998), and the publication of several volumes on issues of diversity, culture, and social justice (e.g., Patton's [1985] *Culture and Evaluation*, Sirotnik's [1990] *Evaluation and Social Justice*, and Madison's [1992] *Minority Issues*).

Despite this initial evaluation literature on social justice and diversity in evaluation, there did not exist deliberate efforts to attract and retain evaluators of color and culturally competent evaluators in the field and profession. The BDI with its focus on improving the quality and effectiveness of evaluation by increasing the number of racially and ethnically diverse

The editors acknowledge the tireless efforts of Karen E. Kirkhart for her incessant attention to detail and the mentoring role she played at the outset of the special issue proposal, Kelly Lane's valuable graphic design support and editorial review, and William Rodick's skill at editing, formatting, and aligning the chapters with appropriate bibliographic referencing.

evaluators in the evaluation profession, and improving the capacity of all evaluators to work across cultures, represented a more purposeful, collaborative, and intensive effort of the AEA to diversify the evaluation profession and serve the societal need for more culturally competent evaluation professionals. The GEDI program emerged out of the recommendations of the BDI. Figure 1 represents the institutional events leading up to development of the BDI and implementation of GEDI. Detailed information on the conception and development of the program is presented in Chapter 1 of this issue by Symonette, Mertens, and Hopson.

For 10 years, the GEDI program has been a viable and sustainable mechanism to build a more inclusive, diverse evaluation field and extend the importance of cultural competence and responsiveness in evaluation. The program aimed to recruit students from diverse racial and ethnic backgrounds into evaluation and to encourage the evaluation field to work in more diverse cultural contexts (Collins & Hopson, 2007; Peak, Peters, & Fishman, 2007). Beyond creating evaluators who may work in diverse contexts, the program worked to develop leaders who are committed to furthering the mission of the AEA, BDI, and contributing to the notions of social justice. To date, the GEDI program has trained 62 graduate students of color from diverse academic disciplines in program evaluation, with 67% of the alumni (41/62) reporting doing program evaluation-related work (Collins, Kirkhart, & Brown, Chapter 2 of this issue). In addition to the 62 alumni, four interns were still in training during the writing of this issue. Since participation in the program, interns have completed graduate and advanced degrees across a spectrum of disciplines such as applied anthropology, psychology (applied social, clinical, development, and public interest), education, family relations/child and family development, public health, language and literacy, law public administration and policy, sociology, social work, and urban planning/studies. What is more, many have continued engagement within AEA, taking on increased leadership roles, such as cochairing Topical Interest Groups (TIGs) and participating in AEA Work Groups. They have published and presented actively both during and following participation in GEDI program.

Overview of the Issue

This issue seeks to address the following questions: (a) what factors contributed to the design and organization of GEDI within AEA? (b) what critical components of the program have been successfully implemented? (c) what is the legacy of the GEDI program thus far? and (d) what lessons have been learned from the program that may influence how internship, leadership, or mentorship experiences may be realized for other professions that attempt similar efforts of expanding pipelines and pathways of diversity and social justice? Ultimately, the issue provides an opportunity for key participants (from leaders to young evaluators of color) of the GEDI

Figure 1. Institutional Events Leading Up to the Development of BDI and Implementation of GEDI

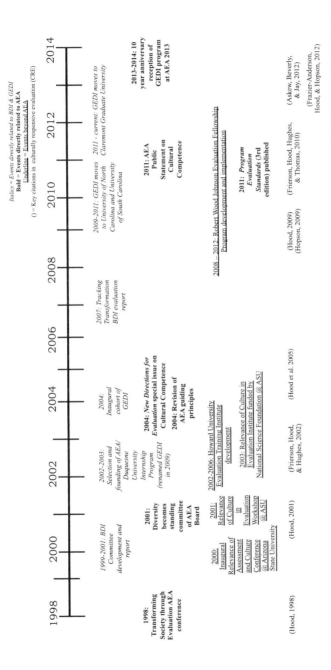

Note: This figure illustrates the various diversification efforts of the AEA and where the GEDI program fits into events directly related to BDI and GEDI. Additionally, the figure depicts diversity events directly related to AEA influence by the BDI, diversity events beyond AEA related to the evaluation profession and field, and key citations in the field related to Culturally Responsive Evaluation (CRE), a key component of the GEDI training curriculum (Collins, Kirkhart, & Brown, Chapter 2 of this issue).

program over the course of the program's development to tell their stories and provide analysis through qualitative and quantitative inquiry.

The contents of this issue emphasize core decisions and developments of the GEDI program and feature key participants who have participated in and contributed to the development and implementation of the program. Together, the chapters focus on the following: (a) factors that contributed to the design and organization of the program; (b) critical components and aspects of the program that guide its implementation, characterized by the leadership training, mentorship and professional socialization, and the practical project placements; and (c) lessons learned that reveal the opportunities and challenges of expanding pipelines and pathways of diversity and social justice through professional associations.

In Chapter 1, Hazel Symonette, Donna M. Mertens, and Rodney Hopson, two instructors during the first several years of the program (Symonette and Mertens) and the founding director (Hopson), provide a unique set of lenses for understanding where the GEDI program has been situated in the field of evaluation and specifically within the American Evaluation Association. Most specifically, their chapter gives a historical background of the GEDI program, providing a glimpse of the organizational power dynamics and debates that led to the birthing of the GEDI program. The authors discuss the circumstances that led up to the decision to begin the BDI, the organizational dynamics of bringing about the changes that BDI and GEDI stimulated in AEA and the evaluation profession, and the implications of this process for AEA's evolution as a culturally responsive organization.

Chapter 2 is authored by two former coordinators (Prisca M. Collins and Tanya Brown) and an instructor (Karen E. Kirkhart). Together, they describe the theoretical framework of the GEDI curriculum. The authors also discuss four levels of intended program outcomes—individual, organizational, community, and professional—and share how the theoretical framework the program adopted guided the development of culturally responsive evaluators committed to social justice and social change. Collins, Kirkhart, and Brown conclude by examining the impact of program participation on the instructors, suggesting pathways of influence that lie outside the original conceptualization of the program and the synergy of evolving Culturally Responsive Evaluation (CRE) theory and GEDI curriculum.

In Chapter 3, Lisa Aponte-Soto, Deborah S. Ling Grant, Frances Carter-Johnson, Soria E. Colomer, Johnavae E. Campbell, and Karen G. Anderson focus on leadership development. As alumni of the program through the Evolution (sixth) cohort, they present findings from a case study of the first six cohorts that they conducted to examine impact of the GEDI program on CRE-related leadership skills. They highlight critical elements of the GEDI program that facilitated the knowledge of transformative leadership skills necessary for advancing CRE and promoting social justice and social change.

In Chapter 4, Ricardo Gomez, Asma Ali, and Wanda Casillas describe how the GEDI program used formal and informal mentoring strategies to facilitate professional growth of the interns and build a strong supportive learning community. As alumni of the Legacy cohort (5), they present findings from a Q methodology inquiry they conducted to examine GEDI intern perspectives on the type of mentorship they received and appropriateness/relevance of the mentoring to their career goals and professional aspirations.

In Chapter 5, authors Michelle L. Bryan and Rita O'Sullivan reflect on their role as codirectors of the GEDI program for the sixth and seventh cohorts, and provide insight into the critical role played by the practical evaluation project experience to support interns' evolving understanding of CRE. By framing the agency internship site as both a pedagogical and a practical space for merging evaluation theory and practice, the authors provide insight into the challenges and processes entailed in training culturally responsive evaluators, and the "value-added" in conducting CRE. Teaching CRE practices involves cultivating a disposition that wholly acknowledges a sociopolitical context. The authors address the ways in which an intern's ability to incorporate tenets of CRE into their work at their internship sites is significantly affected by cultural and contextual factors operating within the internship site, as well as within the programs the interns are helping to evaluate.

Chapter 6 further highlights the critical role mentoring played within the GEDI curriculum. As a "cousin" of the early participants of the program having developed evaluation coursework as a graduate student related to her dissertation on African American evaluators, Tamara Bertrand Jones presents findings from a survey of GEDI alumni discussing the role of the formal and informal mentoring relationships in the socialization of the interns into the evaluation profession. Bertrand Jones emphasizes the importance of both types of mentoring and suggests more effective, complementary ways of using formal and informal mentoring for career development and psychosocial support of interns.

This issue concludes with two chapters that further reflect on the dynamic organizational processes that led to the conception and implementation of the GEDI program, and ponder what all this means 10 years later, and implications for the future. In Chapter 7, Kien Lee and Brandi Gilbert discuss the critical foundational processes and continued efforts put in place to ensure the program continues to grow and advance the social justice agenda. As one of the key administrators of the BDI grant while at the organization then called Association for the Study and Development of Community (now Community Science) (Lee) and one of the participants in the Legacy cohort (5) (Gilbert), they discuss why the internship program is still necessary, but not sufficient for advancing the evaluation profession's role in promoting social justice and equity in the United States. Applying a systems lens to the development of the GEDI program, Lee and Gilbert discuss the challenges and lessons learned through an examination of the program conception and implementation. Ultimately, the chapter is both retrospective and prospective, assessing key context-driven realities of its development and forecasting how an evaluation could stand to benefit from the larger changes that resulted in the program delivery.

Chapter 8 by Stafford Hood serves as a final critique and reflection of the GEDI story. Written as a critical friend, Hood is a leading theorist of CRE and has served as instructor and mentor in the first several years of the program. In his chapter, Hood illuminates the potential legacy of the GEDI program for AEA specifically and the field of evaluation generally. In addition, his critical friend perspectives are fodder for imagining the next 10 years of the program and ways in which evaluation training programs like GEDI serve as harbingers for other important discoveries and innovations in the field and in higher education.

Based on the valuable contributions of the GEDI program to the evaluation profession, the AEA commitment to diversity, and the resources invested by the AEA and other funders, this issue highlights how building diverse leadership can move beyond tokenism to novel development and application of evaluation theory and practice. The GEDI community presents this collaborative effort with the hope that this GEDI training model can serve as an example for academic programs across disciplines, agencies, and leaders in the field who aspire to build leadership skills of emerging evaluators, and for those outside of the field that attempt to build similar models and pathways for practitioners and researchers of color. Finally, we hope that this issue will help evaluators see opportunities to support the next generation of evaluators through the many roles described herein and extend the most successful of training and pathway programs to support a culturally responsive association and profession.

References

American Evaluation Association (AEA). (2011). *American Evaluation Association public statement cultural competence in evaluation.* Retrieved from http://www.eval.org/ccstatement.asp

Askew, K., Beverly, M. G., & Jay, M. L. (2012). Aligning collaborative and culturally responsive approaches, *Evaluation and Program Planning, 35*(4), 552–557.

Collins, P., & Hopson, R. K. (2007). Building leadership development, social justice, and social change in evaluation through a pipeline program. In K. Hannum, J. W. Martineau, & C. Reinelt (Eds.), *The handbook of leadership development evaluation* (pp. 173–198). San Francisco, CA: Jossey-Bass.

Frazier-Anderson, P., Hood, & Hopson, R. (2011). Preliminary considerations of an African American Culturally Responsive Evaluation System. In S. D. Lapan, M. T. Quartaroli, & F. J. Riemer (Eds.), *Qualitative Research: An Introduction to Methods and Designs* (pp. 347–372). San Francisco, CA: Jossey-Bass.

Frierson, H., Hood, S., & Hughes, G. B. (2002). Strategies that address culturally responsive evaluations. In J. Frechtling (Ed.), *The 2002 user-friendly handbook for project evaluation* (p. 63–73). Arlington, VA: National Science Foundation.

Frierson, H. T., Hood, S., Hughes, G. B., & Thomas, V. G. (2010). A guide to conducting culturally-responsive evaluations. In J. Frechtling (Ed.), *The 2010 user-friendly handbook for project evaluation* (pp. 75–96). Arlington, VA: National Science Foundation.

Hood, S. (2001). Nobody knows my name: In praise of African American evaluators who were responsive. In J. C. Greene & T. A. Abma (Eds.), *New Directions for Evaluation: No. 92. Responsive evaluation* (pp. 31–43). San Francisco, CA: Jossey-Bass.

Hood, S. (2009). Evaluation for and by Navajos: A Narrative Case of the Irrelevance of Globalization. In K. Ryan & B. Cousins (Eds.), *The SAGE international handbook of educational evaluation* (pp. 447–464). Thousand Oaks, CA: Sage.

Hood, S., Hopson, R., & Frierson, H. (Eds.). (2005). *The role of culture and cultural context in evaluation: A mandate for inclusion, the discovery of truth and understanding.* New York, NY: Information Age.

Hopson, R. (2009). Reclaiming knowledge at the margins: Culturally responsive evaluation in the current evaluation moment. In K. Ryan & B. Cousins (Eds.), *International handbook on evaluation* (pp. 431–448). Thousand Oaks, CA: Sage.

Kirkhart, K. E. (1995). Seeking multicultural validity: A postcard from the road. *Evaluation Practice, 16*(1), 1–12.

Madison, A.-M. (Ed.). (1992). *New Directions for Program Evaluation: No. 52. Minority issues in program evaluation.* San Francisco, CA: Jossey-Bass.

Patton, M. Q. (Ed.). (1985). *New Directions for Program Evaluation: No. 25. Culture and evaluation.* San Francisco, CA: Jossey-Bass.

Peak, G. I., Peters, L., & Fishman, S. (2007). *Tracking information: Evaluating the American Evaluation Association Building Diversity Initiative.* Report of Phase I evaluation findings. Baltimore, MD: Two Gems Consulting Services.

SenGupta S., Hopson, R., & Thompson-Robinson, M. (2004). Cultural context in evaluation: An overview. In M. Thompson-Robinson, R. K. Hopson, & S. SenGupta (Eds.), *New Directions for Evaluation: No. 102. In search of cultural competence in evaluation: Toward principles and practices* (pp. 5–21). San Francisco, CA: Jossey-Bass.

Sirotnik, K. A. (Ed.). (1990). *New Directions for Program Evaluation: No. 45. Evaluation and social justice: Issues in public education.* San Francisco, CA: Jossey-Bass.

Prisca M. Collins
Rodney Hopson
Editors

PRISCA M. COLLINS *is an assistant professor in the Physical Therapy Program at Northern Illinois University. She served as the inaugural coordinator of the GEDI program from 2004 to 2006.*

RODNEY HOPSON *is a professor in the College of Education and Human Development and a senior research fellow of the Center of Education Policy and Evaluation at George Mason University. He served as founding director of the GEDI program from 2004 to 2009.*

Symonette, H., Mertens, D. M., & Hopson, R. (2014). The development of a diversity initiative: Framework for the Graduate Education Diversity Internship (GEDI) program. In
P. M. Collins & R. Hopson (Eds.), *Building a new generation of culturally responsive evaluators through AEA's Graduate Education Diversity Internship program*. New Directions for
Evaluation, 143, 9–22.

1

The Development of a Diversity Initiative: Framework for the Graduate Education Diversity Internship (GEDI) Program

Hazel Symonette, Donna M. Mertens, Rodney Hopson

Abstract

*The purpose of this chapter is to provide a historical framing for the development
of the American Evaluation Association's (AEA's) Graduate Education Diversity
Internship (GEDI) program as an outgrowth of the AEA's Building Diversity Initiative (BDI). This chapter provides historical documentation of the AEA's BDI
and the origins of the GEDI program and discusses how this represents an important part of AEA's history. We discuss the circumstances that led up to the
decision to begin the BDI, the organizational dynamics of bringing about the
changes that BDI and GEDI stimulated in AEA and the evaluation profession,
and the implications of this process for AEA's evolution as a culturally responsive organization.* © Wiley Periodicals, Inc., and the American Evaluation
Association.

Laying the Groundwork to AEA as a Culturally Responsive Organization

The development of the AEA GEDI initiative was a joint effort of the
American Evaluation Association (AEA) and the W. K. Kellogg Foundation to address the complexity of needs and expectations concerning evaluators working across cultures and in diverse communities (BDI, 2001).
The Building Diversity Initiative (BDI) was guided by the Project Advisory

NEW DIRECTIONS FOR EVALUATION, no. 143, Fall 2014   © 2014 Wiley Periodicals, Inc., and the American Evaluation
Association.   Published online in Wiley Online Library (wileyonlinelibrary.com) • DOI: 10.1002/ev.20090

Committee, cochaired by Donna Mertens and Hazel Symonette, and staffed by David Chavis and Kien Lee of Community Science, formerly the Association for the Study and Development of Community (ASDC). Members of the BDI Advisory Committee were made up of a cross-section of AEA members and nonmembers: leaders, emerging and current, such as Board members, TIG chairs, and others invested in the issues of the BDI.

The purpose of BDI paralleled the mission of the Multi-Ethnic Issues (formerly known as the Minority Issues) in Evaluation (MIE) TIG: (a) to improve the quality and effectiveness of evaluation by increasing the number of racially and ethnically diverse evaluators in the evaluation profession, and (b) to improve the capacity of all evaluators to work across cultures. The BDI was designed to encourage and integrate the comments and perspectives of the AEA Board of Directors and AEA members, as well as other key stakeholders within the evaluation community. The BDI was charged with the following six tasks:

(i) Develop a directory of evaluators;
(ii) Summarize foundation and government agency efforts to identify, increase, and hire evaluators of color;
(iii) Summarize strategies used by other professional organizations to increase diversity;
(iv) Conduct a survey of evaluation training programs;
(v) Develop guiding principles for cross-cultural evaluation; and
(vi) Create a diversity building plan and an evaluation plan.

These six tasks produced the *Evaluator Survey Report, Best Practices Report*, and the *Guiding Principles Subtask Concept Paper.* The results of the BDI's surveys reinforced the need to support the development of training programs for evaluators of color, as Hopson and Collins (2005) report. Those surveys revealed:

> ...a lack of mentoring opportunities, role models, and access to training for evaluators of color. In addition, [ASCD staff] interviewed foundation and federal agency representatives about their engagement with evaluators of color. These interviews exposed the difficulties these institutions face in ensuring culturally responsive evaluations. Respondents attributed this, in part, to the challenge of identifying, accessing, and engaging both evaluators of color and evaluators with the capacity to work with racially and ethnically diverse communities. In fact the majority of the respondents' institutions were not engaged in deliberate efforts to identify diverse evaluators. (p. 1)

Informed by the surveys, BDI's work culminated in the development of 14 recommendations to AEA to increase access and enhance the preparation of evaluators of color in addition to improving the cultural competencies of the larger evaluation community. The first of these recommendations was to create a graduate education fellowship program targeted to students of color. This recommendation provided the basis for what is currently known as the GEDI program. In addition to its diversification agenda, there seemed to be an expectation by leaders of the advisory committee and eventually leaders of the GEDI program that the GEDI program would develop and implement innovative capacity-building curricula and training processes for cultivating socially responsive, socially responsible, and socially just evaluation professionals.

This chapter fills a very important gap in providing a historical record of the Building Diversity Initiative and its implications for the GEDI program. To date, this history has resided in AEA board documentation, minutes, and internal evaluative documents, with very little public record. In addition, with the exception of GEDI program descriptions and intended goals (Collins & Hopson, 2007), little to no published record exists on the processes and framing of the GEDI program from its inception. As the program enters its second decade, this chapter aims to assist evaluation leadership, thought leaders, scholars, and others with ways to build on the foundational framing of the GEDI program.

The layout of the chapter includes a discussion on the methodology that drove the chapter development and results pertaining to the birthing of BDI and GEDI, including key players, tensions, and opportunities or opportunities envisioned nearly a decade ago by three architects of the program.

Methodology

Two primary methods were used to accomplish the purposes of this chapter, i.e., to provide a historical record of the development of BDI and to provide implications for the GEDI program. Initially, we examined documents outlining the deliberations within and among the BDI planning team, the AEA Board, and the W. K. Kellogg Foundation representatives to provide insights into the complex challenges and power dynamics related to diversity change agendas. These deliberative dynamics and developments have been especially germane in the evolution of the GEDI program because of its position among the 14 BDI Recommendations[1] (BDI, 2001). As cochairs of the Building Diversity Initiative (Symonette & Mertens) and first director of the GEDI program (Hopson with support from Prisca Collins, inaugural coordinator), we are in a unique position to describe the progressive change vision of the program. Mertens (former AEA President responsible for the W. K. Kellogg Foundation grant that funded BDI), Symonette (then Co-Chair of the AEA Multi-Ethnic Issues in Evaluation TIG), and Hopson (former Chair of the Multi-Ethnic Issues in Evaluation TIG) served in key roles in the association in moving forward the diversity agenda.

Secondly, we engaged in an audio-recorded and transcribed "trialogue" on two separate occasions in order to reconstruct the history of BDI and discuss the key issues related to the chapter purposes. The trialogue method, an extension of what is more commonly known in the social sciences as dialogue (Frank, 2005; Gildersleeve & Kuntz, 2011; Parsons & Lavery, 2012), was used as an attempt to provide a critical reflection and narrative of the program from the perspectives and experiences of three thought leaders and visionaries of the field. We specifically draw upon our then positions and affiliations in the American Evaluation Association and emerging leadership roles to provide reflective analysis at the time of the BDI development and GEDI implementation. We draw on previous dialogue methods used in evaluation (Abma & Stake, 2001).

We explored questions surrounding the historical framing of BDI focused on our roles and positions in AEA at the time of its development, the role of other key players, key challenges/opportunities that made it possible to develop BDI, and the key organizational and institutional efforts that preceded the development of BDI and GEDI. Questions surrounding the implications of the GEDI development process included issues related to the legacy of GEDI, key lessons learned in AEA about the larger organizational change processes, and the continual development of initiatives in the association and the field to foster diversity.

In the next two sections, we provide excerpts from the trialogue on the historical framing of the GEDI program and implications of the program's development and implementation. Embedded in our trialogue excerpts are additional discussions and observations about key issues and players in the emergence of a more robust diversity agenda in the American Evaluation Association and the evaluation field.

Historical Framing of the GEDI Program

The GEDI program emerged from AEA's Building Diversity Initiative through a process that began with contact from the W. K. Kellogg Foundation and Donna Mertens, AEA's president elect in 1997. The introduction of BDI to AEA's Board and the AEA TIG MIE are documented in this section.

Birthing BDI

The following provides background to the initial discussions that led to the founding of the BDI. Key players in the launch of BDI included the American Evaluation Association, the W. K. Kellogg Foundation, and Community Science (formerly ASDC). The trialogue suggests that birthing of the BDI consisted of bringing together visions of diverse groups of evaluators to develop a cadre of evaluators that were responsive to the needs of underrepresented and underserved groups of color in the United States.

The conception of BDI occurred at a meeting of Mertens, in her role as AEA's president elect in 1997, and Ricardo Millett, the Director of Evaluation at the W. K. Kellogg Foundation at that time. He said that he wanted to talk to Mertens to see if AEA was interested in taking on an initiative to increase diversity in the profession and in the organization. Mertens recalls:

> And of course I said yes. So we sat down there and just talked, you know, really blue sky sort of what could we do, what would it look like, who could be involved.

> As it turned out, he had already floated some ideas with David Chavis at what was then ASDC. …The reason for involving ASDC was based on Ricardo's thinking that this initiative required work that would go beyond the capacity of a volunteer association. I guess the ASDC had done other work for Kellogg, so it was in the same realm and they felt like they had a good relationship. So they wanted to engage them for this scope of work.

> It would be something that would require funding and staff to do the work, but he also wanted it to reflect AEA as the lead so that it would have ties to the profession in a formal way. So with that, he suggested that we get together some players from AEA and from ASDC to talk about what that could look like…

Mertens convened a meeting in Washington, DC, with Millett, Chavis (then AEA Secretary-Treasurer), Charles Thomas, and Edith Thomas (at the time, Chair of AEA's Diversity Committee) to brainstorm what it could look like and what kind of things could be done. From that meeting, a preliminary concept paper was developed focused on what AEA's involvement could be. That concept paper was used as a platform to request the organization to accept the role of playing the lead in developing an initiative to improve diversity in the field of evaluation.

When Mertens took the concept paper to the AEA Board, initial discussions centered on whether AEA was willing to take on this task and if they wanted to accept W. K. Kellogg's conditions in terms of working with ASDC. Mertens recalls:

> I had to really walk that tightrope to say this is something that's worth doing, and this is the mechanism to get it started. It has funds and it has staff, and it's a credible group. So it's not like them coming to us with someone unknown because David (Chavis), at that time, was serving as AEA's treasurer, so he was a very well-known entity.

> So that was a concern, and then the second concern was, should we be focusing just on race. Are there other forms of diversity that would deserve our attention? And, again, personally, I think it was an excellent focus to start with, and, yes, there are other dimensions of diversity.

After extensive discussion, AEA's Board agreed to the development of a full proposal for their consideration that reflected the arrangement outlined in the concept paper. Once the full proposal was developed, it was shared with the Board who approved it. At that point, the BDI was launched and the rollout process began by holding sessions about its intent and activities at the 1999 annual meeting in Orlando. It was at this meeting that it became obvious that important stakeholder groups had not been included in the initial planning of BDI, as is seen in the next section of this chapter.

BDI as a Trojan Horse and the Role of the MIE TIG

The MIE TIG, one of dozens of TIGs of the Association, had long served as an important vehicle in advancing the interests of underserved and traditionally marginalized communities of color and in sensitizing the evaluation field to key inclusive, transformative, and culturally responsive approaches, methods, and epistemologies. The introduction and delivery of the program was viewed with suspicion by the leadership of the MIE TIG because they were not aware of nor involved in its development. It took lengthy and critical discussions between leaders of the TIG and those who proposed the BDI effort to develop a working relationship. Hopson recalls:

> I use this notion as a metaphor, and it's not to suggest that there was anything deliberate or malicious, but it was as if a Trojan horse was coming into the room, and it was laid down before us. I own this statement because in reflection and retrospect, it was as if there was a gift being brought, but no one really knew how that gift was actually going to manifest. But I only say it now in retrospect. I knew we had suspicion about this "gift" of a BDI, and didn't know to what extent that the TIG would be involved since they had not been included in the development of the proposal that was largely focused on issues of diversity in the association.

At that 1999 meeting, Symonette and Ivy Jones Turner were installed as Co-Chairs of the MIE TIG. It was a very contentious time, yet one that we challenged the TIG and those invested in the diversity agenda of the association to transform it into a generative opportunity. Symonette recalls:

> So many brittle suspicions and concerns were swirling as we moved into our first meeting as Co-Chairs. It was very unsettling—in fact, quite scary. I resolved to do my best to hold a robust *grace space* for all voices to be heard yet avoid a total meltdown. I tried to steer clear of dwelling in a blame and shame vortex. It was a very difficult time; however, we needed to clear our communications channels in order to craft a more open, trusting and resilient foundation for living-into BDI's visionary promise.

NEW DIRECTIONS FOR EVALUATION • DOI: 10.1002/ev

Birthing GEDI and the Role of GEDI as Leaders

The BDI recommendation that provided the foundation for the GEDI program was initially conceptualized very narrowly as a fellowship for an individual evaluator of color. The fellowship recommendation was the most challenging one for the AEA Board. It was the only one for which a home could not be located within the existing AEA organizational infrastructure. During its early history, this recommendation was a source of difficult, sometimes heated, Board deliberations. Through those deliberations on the GEDI program, the AEA Board shifted from the more internally resource-intensive fellowship initiative to an internship program. This change had important implications for the development, implementation, and impact of the GEDI program; this will become apparent as the history of the birthing of the GEDI unfolds.

Hopson recalls working with Kien Lee of ASDC to act on the recommendation for an internship. The first step was to develop a prospectus that was disseminated through AEA's network to determine interest in hosting the GEDI. Several proposals were submitted to the AEA Board, one of which was from Hopson; for that reason he recused himself from deliberations about who would provide the first GEDI home. The AEA Board selected Hopson (who hired Prisca Collins as its first coordinator) at Duquesne University to take on that important responsibility, with the proviso that Hopson and his team were responsible for finding funds to support the interns. Hopson provides these reflections on that process:

> I just knew that there were enough people who had worked hard enough on this effort through BDI and previous chairs and so forth, that it was going to happen. I mean there was no doubt in my mind that we would birth a baby that would flourish just because of all the love that there was.

> It was the 2003 AEA conference in Reno that Donna and I met Teri Behrens at W. K. Kellogg Foundation, who was the director of evaluation, who agreed to facilitate the first chunk of money to support the internship program.

Recall the previously mentioned change from fellowship to internship. Symonette was part of what were challenging AEA Board deliberations:

> For a variety of articulated reasons, it was resolved not to support and fund the fellowship recommendation. Instead, the internship concept was advanced as a non-AEA funded initiative. Despite its difficult unfunded birthing, the internship program evolved as a generative opportunity to grow a vibrant community of practice committed to culturally responsive praxis, social justice and transformative change.

Actually, if we had implemented what the recommendation asked for, we would have installed one fellowship per year which would have yielded a *lonely-only* individual navigating new terrain alone. Such a narrowly crafted access agenda would have greatly diminished impact compared to the more expansively generative influence of each GEDI cohort as a mutually-supportive collaborative of learning/development journey partners—a **Posse**-like intervention.

Part of the birthing process of GEDI included a review of what other associations did for fellowships and internships. Hopson wanted to avoid models that provided simply momentary recognition or that provided casual recognition of a group of graduate students at an annual meeting of an association in favor of a model that included deliberate community-building, supportive mechanism of family that supported people across multiple times. And so we wanted to make sure that the internship program had this piece. These were the elements that we knew in building this.

This model for GEDI aligns with the subsequent writings of Meg Wheatley (Wheatley, 2013; Wheatley & Berkana Institute, 2005) on development of leaders through transformative capacity building. Symonette provides this commentary on the connection:

> Thinking about Meg Wheatley's complex systems change work on emergence, I am reminded of her often-quoted mantra: It's not about critical mass but rather about critical connections. By bringing the interns together in collaborative ways, we helped cultivate critical connections. Common interests brought them into GEDI space as they evolved from a network into a community of practice.
>
> There's something that emerges in the middle of those developments—from those individual networking activities towards becoming community. That is what I think happened with the interns over the course of that year. I am sensing that even broader and more robust interconnections are starting to emerge. Moving from networks to communities of practice to systems of influence (Wheately's 3-stage emergent change model).

Wheatley further describes this phenomenon in terms of an emergence (Wheatley & Frieze, 2006):

> Emergence violates so many of our Western assumptions of how change happens that it often takes quite a while to understand it. In nature, change never happens as a result of top-down preconceived strategic plans or from the mandate of any individual or boss. Change begins as local actions spring up simultaneously in many different areas . . . However, when they become connected, local actions can emerge as a powerful system with influence at a more global or comprehensive level.

Wheatley's work illuminates the dynamics behind the transformative process, the development of the core group of people who are focused on action to address injustices and the difficulty of it, and the need to have coordinated action. Symonette extends the application of these concepts in the GEDI strategies for preparing leaders:

> The interns were schooled in—trained and educated in ways that foster expectations that they would not be a bystander to injustice or to evaluation practices that were contrary to contextual and cultural responsiveness. So even if they were not authorized or anointed as the one responsible, they would still find ways to make a difference. In our work, we call this leaderly behavior, in contrast to the more conventional positional leadership.

> Through the internship program, we were growing students for leadership in the conventional way as well as for leaderly behavior in carrying forward, progressive messages wherever they found themselves. They were gaining experiences that they needed to serve as boundary-spanning bridge builders for the greater good.

Implications of BDI and the GEDI: Role of BDI and GEDI in Seeding Other Initiatives in AEA and Beyond

The role of BDI and GEDI had far-reaching implications for the association and field. Initially conceived to develop constructive and transformative processes of leadership and capacity building at the association and individual levels (Collins & Hopson, 2007), the GEDI program has produced 10 cohorts and nearly 65 participants and alumni.

In addition, major changes in guiding documents for evaluators were seeded by the winds of BDI and GEDI. These include AEA's (2011) development of the *Public Statement on Cultural Competence in Evaluation*; revisions of AEA's (2004) *Guiding Principles* to bring greater attention to cultural competence; and the infusion of culture in the *Program Evaluation Standards* (3rd ed.; Yarbrough, Shulha, Hopson, & Caruthers, 2011), not to mention other initiatives such as the Robert Wood Johnson Fellowship Program, which used a similar model influenced by the GEDI program (Christie & Vo, 2011). Hopson commented:

> What's most important to me is that the work from the BDI, from 2001, has seeded a variety of other initiatives and developments in the field and the association. It seeded the Program Evaluation Standards 2nd edition and the cultural reading by the Diversity Committee led by Karen Kirkhart and Melvin Hall (Cultural Reading of the Program Evaluation Standards, 2003). It contributed to the revision of the AEA Guiding Principles, especially a nuanced perspective of culture. These are two major documents that have contributed to how we think about ethical and best practices in the field.

New Directions for Evaluation • DOI: 10.1002/ev

Considering the legacy of GEDI, that story is still worth investigating through an evaluation by the association. GEDI was part of another type of ecological set of changes that took place in systems of transformation that we wouldn't naturally latch onto. While it was unique in itself—I still think there are more stories that still lay untold about how to use CRE (Culturally Responsive Evaluation) in multiple ways (Stokes, Chaplin, Dessouky, Aklilu, & Hopson, 2011)—it was part of a larger system of really repositioning and thinking about the association and how we think about evaluation.

To which Mertens responded:

I started thinking about how the diversity initiative really took an overall cultural change in the organization. And so the internship was one of those manifestations in that it changed the gestalt of thinking, whereas before I don't feel like diversity was on the radar screen in any conscious way. And then through all the work of the people through the years on diversity initiatives and the increased inclusiveness in the board representatives, and the creation of the diversity committee; this was evidence that a shift in the consciousness of the organization to address diversity issues was occurring throughout AEA.

And the question could be raised without any real way to answer it: would the internship program have been successfully endorsed by the organization if it hadn't come at a time when there was momentum? But, really, I mean, my vision of it is a spark coming through and shaking and waking people up and saying there's got to be some real cultural shift throughout the organization of what we attend to. BDI and GEDI represent both a beginning and ongoing momentum for AEA to address issues of diversity in a conscious way—not limited to race—but inclusive of all dimensions of diversity that are used as a basis for discrimination and exclusion.

Symonette's thoughts provide an elegant closure to these reflections on the impact of the BDI and the GEDI on AEA and the evaluation profession:

I think that both BDI and GEDI opened up new and different positive provocative possibilities and opportunities. GEDI cohorts have continued in a generative way to open promising pathways embodied in their presence and the ways they have impacted so many. I use "impact" very broadly, not just in terms of the things that are countable like presentations and leadership positions, but also in the ways in which they move in the world differently with a different kind of portfolio or knapsack than those who have not had that kind of experience. And, most importantly, they share their gifts so that their impact is generative beyond just the boundaries of who are GEDI and who are not.

I think we're seeing it move beyond those boundaries, and so the way was opened for them and then they continue to open the way for others by the way they walk in the world and by the way that people who supported them gaining that new walk were impacted. I think those of us who were sharing in those presentations and trainings were also transformed by them.

So, there was an unleashing of talent and ideas at all stages and phases because it was more emergent and developmental than it was a rollout of a conventional curriculum, where the parameters of the domain were fully known. There was a willingness to allow that to morph through making the path as we walked it. In fact, if we had more robust funding with plenty of strings attached, that kind of generative morphing probably would not have occurred to the extent that it did. And so, that too, was a gift and a blessing.

Postscript

This chapter has explored the historical framing for the development and implementation of the American Evaluation Association's Graduate Education Diversity Internship (GEDI) program, the first recommendation of the Building Diversity Initiative (BDI). The GEDI program was birthed out of larger discussions, movements, and developing literature in the association and the field as a whole. That the GEDI program did not exist in a vacuum is an important observation and reveals how the GEDI program framework required a collaborative effort of leaders and champions in the association. These same leaders and champions developed curricula material for seminars, served as mentors, and provided career development opportunities for GEDI during and after completion of the program. This larger socialization in the program, in the association, and in the field were key components of ways to develop a sustainable structure for developing evaluation leaders through the GEDI program.

Through our transcripted discussion and reflection on the program's developments and implementation, we authors highlight larger issues on the verge of the Association's larger turn and more robust consideration of issues around diversity, race, and culture in the evaluation field. That is, we display the synergies created by BDI and subsequent transformation of the association as a more culturally responsive organization. It is no surprise in reviewing the history of the birthing of GEDI for instance that then current and future Board members and TIG leaders were ensuring that the internal structure of AEA was receptive for the BDI implementation processes. Although GEDI development was the most challenging and arguably the most transformative of the recommendations, the success of the BDI went beyond the development of the GEDI program only (Peak, Peters, & Fishman, 2007). The additional 13 recommendations were as vital to the work of the association as the GEDI recommendation.

NEW DIRECTIONS FOR EVALUATION • DOI: 10.1002/ev

By exploring the larger issues of organizational change, power dynamics, diversity, and cultural responsiveness as groundings for creating and sustaining the GEDI program, at least two goals have been accomplished in this chapter. One goal is intended to provide a historical record of the GEDI program through the reflection and narrative of key thought leaders in the evaluation field. A second goal is to provide insights for others who are interested in pursuing similar efforts related to building and sustaining pipeline and pathway efforts in associations and agencies for years to come. For instance, whereas the GEDI (and BDI) are specific to the organizational and institutional context of the American Evaluation Association, those champions of diversity efforts in other professional associations would be wise to ensure that sufficient practical and scholarly knowledge is understood, as was provided in the BDI through document reviews, surveys, and use of an advisory board. Additionally, champions of diversity in other associations or institutions ought to ensure stakeholders are included and collaborated with in ways that emphasize the benefits of participating individuals and the organization (or field) more generally. In this way, champions of diversity can leverage their full arsenal of support in funding and networking across a variety of levels to ensure the lessons learned from these efforts are deliberate and sustainable.

Appendix

Recommendations of the Building Diversity Initiative for the American Evaluation Association (January 2001).

- *Recommendation 1*—Create a graduate education fellowship program targeted at students of color.
- *Recommendation 2*—Tap into existing educational pipeline programs to expose students of color to evaluation as a career choice.
- *Recommendation 3*—Work with Historically Black Colleges and Universities, Hispanic Serving Institutions, and Tribal Institutions to increase the profile of evaluation as a career choice and to support the creation of evaluation training courses and programs.
- *Recommendation 4*—Create "guaranteed" training sessions at the annual AEA conference to address the professional development needs of evaluators of color and cross-cultural evaluators.
- *Recommendation 5*—Create nontraditional training opportunities for people doing evaluation work, but who do not identify themselves as evaluators.
- *Recommendation 6*—Organize small business development training for evaluators of color who want to start evaluation consulting firms.
- *Recommendation 7*—Provide financial incentives for evaluators of color and all cross-cultural evaluators to participate in professional development and training opportunities.

- *Recommendation 8*—Create a Council of Evaluation Training Programs (CETP) to serve as a forum to discuss issues of diversity and cultural competence as they relate to training and evaluation.
- *Recommendation 9*—Create and promote a "What Is Evaluation?" campaign.
- *Recommendation 10*—Engage in a public education campaign to emphasize the importance of cultural context and diversity in evaluation for evaluation seeking institutions.
- *Recommendation 11*—Incorporate diversity issues into the review of the Program Evaluation Standards.
- *Recommendation 12*—Advocate for the creation of an affirmative hiring policy for foundations and state and local governments.
- *Recommendation 13*—Encourage mentoring for evaluators of color and for those seeking cross-cultural evaluation experience.
- *Recommendation 14*—Work with diverse organizations to publicize job opportunities to evaluators of color.

Note

1. The 14 BDI recommendations were divided into four areas: pipeline, professional development, work access, and recruitment; see the Appendix to this chapter for the full list.

References

Abma, T. A., & Stake, R. E. (2001). Stake's responsive evaluation: Core ideas and evolution. In J. C. Greene & T. A. Abma (Eds.), *New Directions for Evaluation: No. 92. Responsive evaluation* (pp. 7–21). San Francisco, CA: Jossey-Bass.

American Evaluation Association (AEA). (2003). *An introduction to the Cultural Reading of the Program Evaluation Standards* (2nd ed.). Retrieved from http://www.eval.org/p/cm/ld/fid=74

American Evaluation Association (AEA). (2004). *AEA guiding principles.* Retrieved from http://www.eval.org/p/cm/ld/fid=51

American Evaluation Association (AEA). (2011). *AEA public statement on cultural competence.* Retrieved from http://www.eval.org/p/cm/ld/fid=92

Building Diversity Initiative (BDI). (2001). *The building diversity plan.* Gaithersburg, MD: Association for the Study and Development of Communities.

Christie, C. A., & Vo, A. T. (2011). Promoting diversity in the field of evaluation: Reflections on the first year of the Robert Wood Johnson Foundation Evaluation Fellowship Program. *American Journal of Evaluation, 32*(4), 547–564. doi:10.1177/1098214011399644

Collins, P., & Hopson, R. (2007). Building leadership development, social justice, and social change in evaluation through a pipeline program. In K. Hannum, J. W. Martineau, & C. Reinelt (Eds.), *The handbook of leadership development evaluation* (pp. 173–198). San Francisco, CA: Jossey-Bass.

Frank, A. W. (2005). What is dialogical research, and why should we do it? *Qualitative Health Research, 15*(7), 964–974.

Gildersleeve, R. E., & Kuntz, A. M. (2011). A dialogue on space and method in qualitative research on education. *Qualitative Inquiry, 17*(1), 15–22.

Hopson, R., & Collins, P. (2005). Building a pipeline for evaluators of color. *The Evaluation Exchange*, *11*(2), 1.

Parsons, J. A., & Lavery, J. V. (2012). Brokered dialogue: A new research method for controversial health and social issues. *BMC Medical Research Methodology*, *12*(1), 92.

Peak, G. L., Peters, L., & Fishman, S. (2007). *Tracking transformation: Evaluating the American Evaluation Association Building Diversity Initiative*. Report of Phase I evaluation findings. Baltimore, MD: Two Gems Consulting Services.

Stokes, H., Chaplin, S., Dessouky, S., Aklilu, L., & Hopson, R. (2011). Serving marginalized populations through culturally responsive evaluation. *Diaspora, Indigenous, and Minority Education*, *5*(3), 167–177.

Wheatley, M. J. (2013, June 6). Lost and found in a brave new world. *Leader to Leader*, *68*, 46–51.

Wheatley, M. J., & Berkana Institute. (2005). *It's about time*. Spokane, WA: Berkana Institute.

Wheatley, M. J., & Frieze, D. (2006). *Using emergence to take social innovations to scale*. Retrieved from http://www.margaretwheatley.com/articles/emergence.html

Yarbrough, D., Shulha, L. M., Hopson, R., & Caruthers, F. (2010). *The program evaluation standards: A guide for evaluators and evaluation users* (3rd ed.). Thousand Oaks, CA: Sage.

HAZEL SYMONETTE is program development and assessment specialist in the Division of Student Life at the University of Wisconsin-Madison, Madison, WI. In her role as Co-Chair of the Minority Issues in Evaluation Topical Interest Group, she served for three years as the initial Co-Chair of BDI until elected to the AEA Board.

DONNA M. MERTENS is editor of the Journal of Mixed Methods Research *and a retired professor from the Department of Education at Gallaudet University, Washington, DC. She shepherded the BDI from the beginning conversations with W. K. Kellogg Foundation to its conclusion, serving as Co-Chair throughout the implementation of the initiative.*

RODNEY HOPSON is a professor in the College of Education and Human Development and a senior research fellow of the Center of Education Policy and Evaluation at George Mason University. He served as founding director of the GEDI program from 2004 to 2009.

Collins, P. M., Kirkhart, K. E., & Brown, T. (2014). Envisioning an evaluation curriculum to develop culturally responsive evaluators and support social justice. In P. M. Collins & R. Hopson (Eds.), *Building a new generation of culturally responsive evaluators through AEA's Graduate Education Diversity Internship program. New Directions for Evaluation, 143*, 23–36.

2

Envisioning an Evaluation Curriculum to Develop Culturally Responsive Evaluators and Support Social Justice

Prisca M. Collins, Karen E. Kirkhart, Tanya Brown

Abstract

This chapter describes the theoretical framework underlying the Graduate Education Diversity Internship (GEDI) program curriculum and discusses how the program evolved over time. It describes the various components of the program, plus factors that influenced curriculum content and format. The chapter also discusses four levels of intended program outcomes: individual, organizational, community, and professional. As former coordinators and instructor of the program, we explain how the theoretical framework we adopted guided the development of culturally responsive evaluators committed to social justice and social change. The chapter concludes by examining the impact of program participation on the instructors, suggesting pathways of influence that lie outside the original conceptualization of the program, including how the synergy of evolving theory and curriculum enriched the program. © Wiley Periodicals, Inc., and the American Evaluation Association.

Program Conception

The GEDI program was created as part of the American Evaluation Association's (AEA's) efforts to address the recommendations of the AEA Building

The authors wish to thank Mark Collins, EdD, Oswego, IL, and Kelly D. Lane, MSW, Syracuse, NY, for their rendering of Figure 2.1.

Diversity Initiative (BDI). The BDI recommended that the AEA increase the number of evaluators of color and improve the capacities of all evaluators to work effectively across cultures (BDI, 2001). The GEDI program enrolled its first cohort in 2004. The goals of the program were to (a) recruit graduate students of color from diverse fields so as to extend their research capacities to evaluation; (b) stimulate evaluation thinking concerning diverse communities and persons of color; and (c) deepen the evaluation profession's capacity to work in racially, ethnically, and culturally diverse settings (Collins & Hopson, 2007). The curriculum of the program was developed with these goals in mind, and shaped by the efforts and ideas leading to its initial conception.

Curriculum Framework

The GEDI program curriculum framework was developed based on theories of social justice and social change within evaluation literature, with attention to underserved and unrecognized populations (Collins & Hopson, 2007). Social justice refers to assessing whether institutions of a society are arranged to produce appropriate, fair, and moral distributions of benefits and burdens among its members and groups (Mathison, 2005). Barry MacDonald (1976) and Ernest House (1980, 1990) were among the first to connect the importance of social justice with evaluation (Thomas & Madison, 2010). Evaluation of social and educational programs, and contextual politics, have direct impacts on the very groups the programs serve. When evaluators are anchored by the aims of social justice, their activities are conceptualized with explicit consideration of the impact of a particular program on a social system. Without these considerations, social programs, and the evaluators who assess them, risk becoming complicit with existing inequities and contributing to barriers to accessing resources for these communities.

It is not enough for evaluators to possess a theoretical and methodological knowledge of socially just practices. They also must demonstrate an ability to relate to various stakeholders in a respectful manner. They must facilitate trusting relationships, think critically, and be responsive to a diversity of voices, especially voices of those traditionally marginalized. Evaluators should reflexively consider how their positions within a particular context and their own values may shape the decisions that they make.

Program Participants

Students admitted into the GEDI program came from diverse academic disciplines and were required to have foundational knowledge of research methods and substantive issues in their fields of expertise prior to acceptance into the program. Table 2.1 provides a listing of the GEDI cohorts, numbers in each cohort, and the universities that hosted them. During each

Table 2.1. American Evaluation Association Graduate Education Diversity Internship (GEDI) Cohort Numbers and Host University

Cohort Number	Academic Year	Cohort Size	Host University
1	2004–2005	4	Duquesne University
2	2005–2006	4	Duquesne University
3	2006–2007	8	Duquesne University
4	2007–2008	9	Duquesne University
5	2008–2009	7	Duquesne University
6	2009–2010	9	University of North Carolina–Chapel Hill and University of South Carolina
7	2010–2011	8	University of North Carolina–Chapel Hill and University of South Carolina
8	2011–2012	7	Claremont Graduate University
9	2012–2013	6	Claremont Graduate University
10	2013–2014	4	Claremont Graduate University

of the first two years, four interns were accepted and enrolled into the program; however, with extra funding from the National Science Foundation, the program increased enrollment to eight interns in the third year. Enrollment ranged from seven to nine interns from year 4 to year 8, but then dropped to six and four in the 9th and 10th years, respectively, due to challenges locating suitable intern placement sites within a reasonable commuting distance. The number of interns enrolled each year varied based on the number of agencies willing to sponsor an intern and the hosting university's capacity. The GEDI program as of January 2014 has 62 alumni and 4 currently enrolled interns.

Criteria for entry into the program included the following: being a graduate student of color whose academic focus was not evaluation; fit of intern's academic schedule and professional goals with internship goals; ability to meet required time commitment; capacity of intern to successfully complete the program; articulation of how the internship experience would inform intern's area of academic focus; and willingness of a faculty member from the intern's school to serve as an academic advisor during the internship. Because the interns were expected to already have expertise in quantitative research methods and in areas of their academic/professional discipline prior to admission, the program focused on equipping them with knowledge and skills in evaluation and qualitative methods, and providing supportive mechanisms to enhance their confidence as evaluators. The program also aimed at strengthening the interns' ability to contribute to the discourse about issues pertaining to multiculturalism in evaluation and empowerment of communities of color. This was all intended to deepen the intern's understanding of the challenges facing racially, ethnically, and culturally diverse populations.

NEW DIRECTIONS FOR EVALUATION • DOI: 10.1002/ev

GEDI Curriculum Components

The GEDI curriculum consisted of two main components: instructional modalities and leadership development activities. Figure 2.1 illustrates the inputs, components, and outcomes of the GEDI program.

Instructional Modalities

The first component consisted of three instructional modalities: (a) evaluation seminars at the host university, (b) professional development workshops through the AEA/Center for Disease Control (CDC) Summer Institute and AEA pre- and postconference workshops, and (c) practical evaluation project placements with sponsoring agencies. The seminars and the workshops were designed to produce knowledge and skills in evaluation in general and in Culturally Responsive Evaluation (CRE) in particular. Each intern was placed with a sponsoring agency for nine months to design and conduct an evaluation of relevance to the agency. Weekly time commitments for onsite evaluation work (not to exceed 20 hours a week) varied for each intern based on the sponsoring agency, type of evaluation project, and intern's academic schedule.

The evaluation seminars, workshops, and practical evaluation project placements were designed to inform each other. Peer interactions and discussions with senior mentors during the evaluation seminars and workshops provided opportunities for interns to reflect on their evaluation projects and gain further knowledge or insight about how to address issues arising on the evaluation site. The interns also received one-on-one coaching on their evaluation projects from senior evaluators during the seminars. Senior evaluators included past and current AEA presidents and board members, university professors who teach evaluation, and government-level evaluation officers. The seminars provided instruction on introductory evaluation concepts (e.g., history, logic models, role of stakeholders, implementing evaluation), CRE theory, and qualitative research methods. Presentations during the evaluation seminars were delivered by senior evaluators who had been pivotal in advancing CRE theory and in advancing notions of social justice in evaluation.

Even though the core instructional curriculum components of the GEDI program remained consistent over the first 10 years of the program, the length of the evaluation seminars at the host university ranged in duration from 3 to 5 days, depending on intern professional needs, practical placement project evaluation knowledge needs, GEDI program funding, and/or host university resources or preferences. The interns selected the types of workshops to attend at AEA annual conferences or AEA/CDC Summer Institute based on their educational and professional needs. The seminar speakers also varied depending on host university preferences and intern needs, but the focus remained on dissemination of CRE and social

Figure 2.1. Assumptions Underlying the GEDI Curriculum

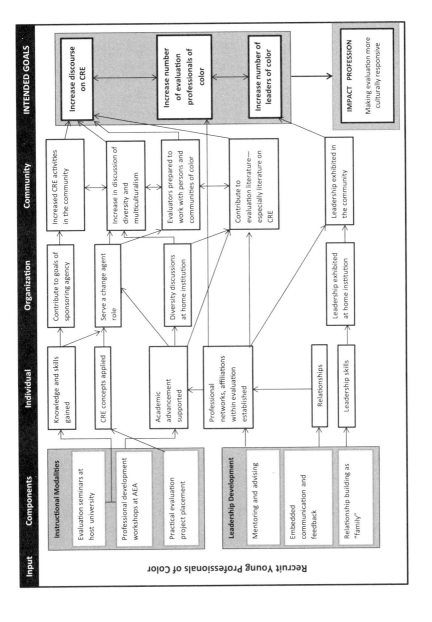

justice in evaluation knowledge, and development of qualitative research skills.

The types of practical evaluation projects in which the interns engaged were determined by the interests and needs of the various stakeholders (AEA, private foundations, nonprofit agencies, community-based organizations) who were willing to sponsor interns located in their geographical areas. During years 3, 4, and 5 of the GEDI program, with extra funding from the National Science Foundation, the curriculum was broadened to address ways that CRE can be applied to programs serving the needs of Science, Technology, Engineering, and Mathematics (STEM) fields. The curriculum then returned to its traditional track of equipping the interns with qualitative inquiry and evaluation skills to conduct CREs across diverse settings during the 6th year.

Leadership Development Activities

The second component of the curriculum consisted of leadership development activities, including: (a) mentoring and advising; (b) embedded communication channels and feedback loops; and (c) community/relationship building among the interns, and between interns and GEDI program administrators and mentors (see Figure 2.1). Interns received mentorship from senior evaluators, GEDI staff, and practical evaluation project on-site supervisors. The type and intensity of mentorship depended on intern needs, mentor availability, and GEDI staff determination of type of intern support needed. Mentorship approaches varied significantly among interns (Bertrand Jones, Chapter 6 of this issue; Gómez, Ali, & Casillas, Chapter 4 of this issue).

During the course of the internship, the interns also received academic advising from a faculty advisor at the university where they were enrolled. This was necessary to ensure that the interns remained on track with their academic work. The faculty advisor also served as a point of contact for the GEDI staff to address academic-related issues arising during the course of the internship.

Embedded communication channels included use of social media, interactive educational platforms (such as blackboard), intern journaling, and telephone availability of GEDI staff. Over the 10 years of the program, the various cohorts had opportunity to attend onsite presentations at major government departments that included the National Science Foundation (NSF) and Government Accountability Office (GAO) and Performance Measurement and Evaluation sector of the Treasury Board in the Canadian Ministry of Finance. They also attended networking events offered at AEA conferences such as the graduate student career and networking workshops, AEA Minority Serving faculty events, AEA pipeline task force meetings, dinner events with AEA board members, and GEDI commencement ceremonies.

New Directions for Evaluation • DOI: 10.1002/ev

During the course of the internship, the interns were encouraged to keep journals wherein they documented personal evaluation journeys. The journaling provided an avenue for the interns to reflect on cultural and power dynamics occurring at the program being evaluated. The interns also reflected on how they negotiated their roles as evaluators and the roles of their mentors and/or advisors during this process. It was expected that the reflections from the journal would be valuable information that the interns could use in their careers as evaluators and also possibly act as notes for future manuscript generation, civic engagement, and/or coaching of upcoming evaluators. The interns presented papers and networked with colleagues and leaders in evaluation and other fields during the AEA annual conferences and the AEA/CDC Summer Institute.

The interns also had the opportunity to interact and share experiences of their evaluation journey with past cohorts through social media and in person during the evaluation conferences. Since the interns came from diverse disciplines and institutions, they brought a rich variety of information and experiences to the dialogue held at the conferences, seminars, and through social media. The interns were encouraged to apply knowledge from their respective disciplines and allow differences to enrich the discussions. The discussions over social media and interactive educational technology and at conferences created an active learning community for brainstorming about collaborative scholarly work and social issues related to communities of color. The collaboration on this *New Directions for Evaluation* issue is evidence of the vibrancy of the GEDI learning community.

The multiple modes of communication embedded into GEDI curriculum allowed for regular updates and feedback to and from the interns and GEDI staff and facilitated building strong relationships. The intensive mentoring and relationship-building activities, combined with the multiple communication channels, were intended to help the interns form a cohesive group identity that bonded them, their leaders, and members of other GEDI cohorts as "family," with the common goal of championing the voices of the traditionally marginalized populations and becoming agents of social change in evaluation.

The leadership development model adopted by the GEDI program was inspired by the ideas of social justice within evaluation and reflected adherence to leadership development principles such as those proposed by Connaughton, Lawrence, and Ruben (2003). Connaughton et al. (2003) state that "leadership competencies are best developed over time through a program that fosters personalized integration of theory and practice and conceives leadership development as a recursive and reflective process" (p. 46).

Together, instructional modalities and leadership development activities intertwined to support learning outcomes. The instructional methods used aimed at delivering the expected program outcomes and providing interns with avenues to put the theory they learned into practice and to reflect on the consequences of their actions through journaling and discussions with mentors and peers. The interns would then use what they gain from the reflections and discussions to further refine the evaluation projects they were engaged in. This process repeated itself throughout the intern's journey through GEDI.

Intended Outcomes of the GEDI Program

Figure 2.1 illustrates expected outcomes of the GEDI program at the individual, organizational, and community levels and the various pathways through which the program components were designed to contribute to the attainment of the outcomes.

Outcomes Related to the Instructional Modalities

The instructional modalities (evaluation seminars, professional development workshops, and practical evaluation projects) were intended to equip the interns with evaluation knowledge and skills (individual level outcomes) and this would in turn enable the interns to contribute to the goals of the sponsoring agency (organization level), while exploring the interface with CRE in working with the community being evaluated (community level). Knowledge and skills gained, combined with the application of CRE concepts during the practical evaluation project placement, were expected to position the interns in a change-agent role as they raised issues framed by CRE in the agency context. This in turn would serve to promote discussion of issues related to diversity and multiculturalism within the evaluation profession and beyond. It would also prepare interns to work effectively with diverse communities of color, and in so doing, meet the intended program goal of increasing the discourse around CRE in the evaluation profession and broader educational and professional communities.

The instructional modalities were also expected to enhance the intern's academic development and ability to serve in the role of change agent. Enhanced academic development positions the intern to engage in discussion of issues of diversity and multiculturalism at the intern's academic institution and also prepares the intern to contribute to evaluation literature, especially the literature on CRE. All of these activities and the presence of these new evaluators of color in the community were expected to increase the discourse on CRE, along with increasing the number of evaluation professionals of color, and positively impact the evaluation profession, making it more culturally responsive.

Outcomes Related to Leadership Development Activities

The leadership development activities (mentoring and advising, embedded communication and feedback, and relationship building as "family") were intended to build leadership skills. These leadership skills were intended to

NEW DIRECTIONS FOR EVALUATION • DOI: 10.1002/ev

equip the interns to take on leadership roles at their home institutions. Empowered by the networks formed among interns, GEDI staff, and mentors, the interns would be an integral part of the evaluation community and feel supported and confident enough to engage in scholarly work and to sign up for leadership positions within AEA and in the community. Collectively, these outcomes were expected to facilitate the attainment of the core goal of increasing leaders of color in the profession.

Attainment of the Intended Goals of the GEDI Program

The program celebrated its 10th anniversary at the annual AEA conference in October of 2013. During this time of celebration, the program had 62 alumni and 4 current predoctoral interns. All intended components of the internship program were fully implemented. The program has consistently had a university to host it and has received funding and support from the AEA and diverse sponsoring agencies throughout the 10 years. The GEDI program has maintained a good collaborative relationship with the AEA to ensure that interns are well supported and receive adequate professional development to build their program evaluation portfolios.

Most GEDI alumni maintain contact with the program staff with whom they worked, as staff members continue to serve as informal mentors, guiding interns through career decisions and writing reference letters as needed. The GEDI program staff sent out a request for employment updates to all GEDI alumni from the first seven cohorts and received updates from 41 of the 49 alumni. Forty of the alumni reported holding positions in program evaluation or research in government, universities, research centers, and research and evaluation firms and associations; taught content related to culture/diversity issues; or were completing graduate degrees in policy and public health at both predominately White and historically Black colleges and universities in the United States. In addition to a wide variety of social sciences represented by the first seven cohorts from across the country, cohorts were made up of African American, Latino/a, Native American, and Asian American predoctoral students.

Consistent with the CRE premises on which the GEDI curriculum is based, the program has engaged in continuous reflection and self-evaluation conducted by the interns and the GEDI staff. While enrolled in the program, the interns engaged in formative evaluation processes of the internship by completing surveys, participating in focus groups, sharing some of their evaluation journal entries or conducting interviews of other cohorts. Surveys and focus groups were conducted during the first two years of the program. Findings revealed that interns felt competent to apply basic evaluation theories during practical evaluation placements and to negotiate their roles as evaluators. Further, they reported confidence in their abilities to engage multiple stakeholders, ensuring that all voices are heard throughout the evaluation process, and paying attention to issues of multicultural validity. As former coordinators of the GEDI program, Collins and Brown observed firsthand the strong personal and professional relationships that developed among the interns, and between interns, GEDI staff, and the various senior evaluators who served as mentors. These relationships were evident through collaborative efforts to generate and present papers at AEA annual conferences and invitations to attend AEA board dinners or lunches during the AEA annual meetings.

Unintended Emerging Outcomes of the GEDI Program

While the GEDI program clearly was aimed at supporting a pipeline of young evaluators of color, the ultimate goal supported by GEDI of making the evaluation *profession* more culturally responsive reflexively impacted the instructors as well. Although instructors were invited to lecture and/or to mentor based upon their established areas of expertise and bodies of work, their own professional development continued. Instructors themselves were changed through their GEDI participation, enabling them to bring new perspectives to their leadership roles within the profession. Their professional status and leadership in turn supported the cultural responsiveness of the profession as a whole. These "recoil effects" (Scriven, 1991, p. 303) impacting instructors clearly illustrate the power of unintended outcomes. Six specific types of influence on instructors are visible in the GEDI program: challenging assumptions, testing and refining theory, translating theory into practice, learning alongside interns, networking among colleagues, and building intergenerational relationships.

Challenging Assumptions

When one is asked basic questions about one's work, it challenges complacency and sharpens thinking to be able to give clear responses in plain language, stripped of the trappings of jargon and assumptions within one's own profession or academic discipline. For example, Kirkhart teaches in a School of Social Work, a setting that explicitly values diversity and infuses it in all aspects of the curriculum. This can lead to a certain complacency of unexamined assumptions when one is "preaching to the choir" of like-minded individuals with substantially similar values. Having GEDI interns come from a range of disciplines and pose questions and challenges led instructors to sharpen their responses and to examine multidisciplinary perspectives.

Testing and Refining Theory

The implementation of GEDI was uniquely positioned alongside the development of CRE theory itself (Askew, Beverly, & Jay, 2012; Frazier-Anderson, Hood, & Hopson, 2012; Frierson, Hood, & Hughes, 2002; Frierson, Hood, Hughes, & Thomas, 2010; Hood, 1998, 2001, 2009; Hopson, 2009), and there was a synergy between the two as they moved in tandem toward the common professional goal of building a more culturally responsive evaluation profession. In seminars, instructors often accompanied presentations on theoretical work with application exercises to link theory to the interns' ongoing projects. Interns' responses and questions revealed areas of unclarity or tension that in turn led instructors to reflect on and refine the theories. For example, when Kirkhart interacted with interns on an Integrated Theory of Influence (Kirkhart, 2000), it helped center influence as an integral part of evaluation and draw out the intersection with leadership skills. With respect to multicultural validity (Kirkhart, 1995, 2005, 2010; LaFrance, Kirkhart, & Nichols, forthcoming), intern responses helped focus on intersectionality and seek simpler ways of portraying and explaining theory.

Translating Theory Into Practice

The applied nature of the GEDI program challenged instructors to translate ideology and theory into principles of practice. While theory was welcomed, the "so what?" question was ever present, pressing instructors to clarify how their ideas and understandings translated into action, making a difference in interns' behavior. These demands of the GEDI instructional context helped to advance the theory and practice of CRE.

Learning Alongside Interns

The early structure of the program invited multiple instructors onsite at one time, so they were exposed to one another's content and often invited to participate in a curriculum unit as a learner. Instructors also participated in field trips (e.g., National Science Foundation) that imparted new knowledge and established a collegial relationship among GEDI interns and instructors. Moving instructors into the direct consumer role added benefit by supporting cross-referencing of content across lectures and experiences as well as providing new skills and knowledge to the instructors themselves.

Networking Among Colleagues

Professional collaborations emerged through GEDI instructor interactions that led to publishing opportunities, copresenting other workshops, consultation on funded research, and collaboration on service projects that advance CRE. Examples include the published work of Hopson, Kirkhart, and Bledsoe (2012) and Mertens (2012) on equity-focused evaluation, and workshops conducted at the AEA/CDC Summer Institute by Mertens and Bledsoe, and Hopson and Kirkhart, and at Claremont Graduate University by Hopson and Casillas.

Building Intergenerational Relationships

Many of the GEDI instructors were selected for their senior role in the profession, having held office(s) within AEA and published widely in the evaluation literature. To support a continuing focus on social justice in the profession, it is important that "elders" build relationships with new generations of evaluators, allowing "elders" to continue to mentor, to nominate their younger colleagues' accomplishments for recognition, and to connect them with relevant leadership positions in AEA. The camaraderie among interns and instructors promoted by the social interactions and events of the GEDI program (e.g., a group meal at a local restaurant or a performing arts event) supported continuing professional relationships across diversity of age and experience.

Conclusion

Creating an evaluation profession that is culturally responsive is an expansive project that spans theory development, evaluation practice, and professional education. It is ambitious work. GEDI responded to a portion of this work by creating a pipeline of skilled young evaluators of color, well prepared to change the face of the profession and to provide leadership in centering evaluation in culture. The curriculum was carefully constructed to balance instructional activities and leadership development; each of the elements within these two components was necessary but insufficient. Collectively, the relative emphasis that emerged was specific to the needs and talents of each GEDI cohort and of each member within a cohort. For example, one cohort might have a stronger "family" identification than another. One member might learn primarily from didactic instruction, while for another, the practical project was the pivotal learning experience. Though Figure 2.1 portrays the overall logic of the curriculum, the story of each intern's move toward advancing the profession's cultural responsiveness might appear different.

Even though the directorship or management of the GEDI program rotated through three host universities (Duquesne University, University of North Carolina-Chapel Hill/University of South Carolina, and Claremont Graduate University), the program remained true to its mission of recruiting graduate students of color and preparing them to be evaluators through the use of instructional modalities (evaluation seminars, professional development workshops, and practical evaluation project placements) and the application of leadership development principles (mentoring and advising, communication feedback loops, and relation building as "family"). The program was fully implemented and remains sustainable due to the commitment of the AEA leadership and the evaluation community at large who continue to provide funding, and serve as mentors and sponsoring agencies for the interns.

NEW DIRECTIONS FOR EVALUATION • DOI: 10.1002/ev

The unwavering commitment of the GEDI directors and coordinators to raising a new generation of culturally responsive evaluators who are passionate to serve as change agents greatly contributed to the viability of the program over the years, and facilitated stronger bonds between members of the GEDI "family." This bonding was also facilitated by the lived experiences of the interns who were members of communities of color and/or traditionally marginalized groups. The program selected interns who were a good fit with the program goals and who could clearly articulate (in writing during the application process) how the internship would inform their academic and professional aspirations. These interns already had a passion for issues of multiculturalism and diversity; hence, the main task of the program was to guide them toward considering program evaluation as a valuable tool to add to their academic and professional portfolios. All these factors distinguish the GEDI program as a community-oriented program that is committed to empowering traditionally marginalized populations and challenging the evaluation profession to be culturally responsive.

References

Askew, K., Beverly, M. G., & Jay, M. (2012). Aligning collaborative and culturally responsive evaluation approaches. *Evaluation and Program Planning, 35*(4), 552–557.

Building Diversity Initiative (BDI). (2001). *The building diversity plan.* Gaithersburg, MD: Association for the Study and Development of Communities.

Collins, P., & Hopson, R. K. (2007). Building leadership development, social justice, and social change in evaluation through a pipeline program. In K. Hannum, J. W. Martineau, & C. Reinelt (Eds.), *The handbook of leadership development in evaluation* (pp. 173–198). San Francisco, CA: Jossey-Bass.

Connaughton, S. L., Lawrence, F. L., & Ruben, B. D. (2003). Leadership development as a systematic and multidisciplinary enterprise. *Journal of Education for Business, 79*(1), 46–51.

Frazier-Anderson, P., Hood, S., & Hopson, R. K. (2012). Preliminary consideration of an African American Culturally Responsive Evaluation System. In S. Lapan, M. Quartaroli, & F. Riemer (Eds.), *Qualitative research: An introduction to methods and designs* (pp. 347–372). San Francisco, CA: Jossey-Bass.

Frierson, H. T., Hood, S., & Hughes, G. B. (2002). Strategies that address culturally-responsive evaluation. In J. Frechtling (Ed.), *The 2002 user-friendly handbook for project evaluation* (pp. 63–73). Arlington, VA: National Science Foundation.

Frierson, H. T., Hood, S., Hughes, G. B., & Thomas, V. G. (2010). A guide to conducting culturally-responsive evaluations. In J. Frechtling (Ed.), *The 2010 user-friendly handbook for project evaluation* (pp. 75–96). Arlington, VA: National Science Foundation.

Hood, S. (1998). Responsive evaluation Amistad style: Perspectives of one African American evaluator. In R. Davis (Ed.), *Proceedings of the Stake symposium on educational evaluation* (pp. 101–112). Urbana-Champaign: University of Illinois.

Hood, S. (2001). Nobody knows my name: In praise of African American evaluators who were responsive. In J. C. Greene & T. A. Abma (Eds.), *New Directions for Evaluation: No. 92. Responsive evaluation* (pp. 31–44). San Francisco, CA: Jossey-Bass.

Hood, S. (2009). Evaluation for and by Navajos: A narrative case of the irrelevance of globalization. In K. E. Ryan & J. B. Cousins (Eds.), *The SAGE international handbook of educational evaluation* (pp. 447–463). Thousand Oaks, CA: Sage.

Hopson, R. K. (2009). Reclaiming knowledge at the margins: Culturally responsive evaluation in the current evaluation moment. In K. Ryan & J. B. Cousins (Eds.), *The SAGE international handbook of educational evaluation* (pp. 429–446). Thousand Oaks, CA: Sage.

Hopson, R. K., Kirkhart, K. E., & Bledsoe, K. B. (2012). Decolonizing evaluation in a developing world: Implications and cautions for Equity-Focused Evaluations (EFE). In M. Segone (Ed.), *Evaluation for equitable development results* (pp. 59–82). New York, NY: UNICEF.

House, E. (1980). *Evaluation with validity.* Thousand Oaks, CA: Sage.

House, E. (1990). Methodology and justice. In K. Sirotnik (Ed.), *New Directions for Program Evaluation: No. 45. Evaluation and social justice: Issues in education* (pp. 23–36). San Francisco, CA: Jossey-Bass.

Kirkhart, K. E. (1995). Seeking multicultural validity: A postcard from the road. *Evaluation Practice, 16*(1), 1–12.

Kirkhart, K. E. (2000). Reconceptualizing evaluation use: An integrated theory of influence. In V. J. Caracelli & H. Preskill (Eds.), *New Directions for Evaluation: No. 88. The expanding scope of evaluation use* (pp. 5–23). San Francisco, CA: Jossey-Bass.

Kirkhart, K. E. (2005). Through a cultural lens: Reflections on validity and theory in evaluation. In S. Hood, R. K. Hopson, & H. T. Frierson (Eds.), *The role of culture and cultural context: A mandate for inclusion, the discovery of truth, and understanding in evaluative theory and practice* (pp. 21–39). Greenwich, CT: Information Age.

Kirkhart, K. E. (2010). Eyes on the prize: Multicultural validity and evaluation theory. *American Journal of Evaluation, 31*(3), 400–413.

LaFrance, J., Kirkhart, K. E., & Nichols, R. (forthcoming). Cultural views of validity: A conversation. In S. Hood, R. K. Hopson, K. Obeidat, & H. Frierson (Eds.), *Continuing the journey to reposition culture and cultural context in evaluation theory and practice.* Greenwich, CT: Information Age.

MacDonald, B. (1976). Evaluation and the control of education. In D. Tawney (Ed.), *Curriculum evaluation today: Trends and implications* (pp. 125–136). London, UK: Macmillan.

Mathison, S. (Ed.). (2005). *Encyclopedia of evaluation.* Thousand Oaks, CA: Sage.

Mertens, D. M. (2012). When human rights is the starting point for evaluation. In M. Segone (Ed.), *Evaluation for equitable development results* (pp. 25–38). New York, NY: UNICEF.

Scriven, M. (1991). *Evaluation thesaurus.* Newbury Park, CA: Sage.

Thomas, V. G., & Madison, A. (2010). Integration of social justice into the teaching of evaluation. *American Journal of Evaluation, 31*(4), 570–583. doi:10.1177/1098214010368426

PRISCA M. COLLINS *is an assistant professor in the Physical Therapy Program at Northern Illinois University. She served as the inaugural coordinator of the GEDI program from 2004 to 2006.*

KAREN E. KIRKHART *is a professor in the School of Social Work, Syracuse University, Syracuse, New York. She served on the Advisory Board of the Building Diversity Initiative and instructed and mentored in the GEDI program from 2005 to 2009.*

TANYA BROWN *is the Residential Life Program Coordinator and staff psychologist at University of California, Los Angeles' Counseling and Psychological Services (CAPS). She served as coordinator of the GEDI program from 2006 to 2007.*

Aponte-Soto, L., Ling Grant, D. S., Carter-Johnson, F., Colomer, S. E., Campbell, J. E., & Anderson, K. G. (2014). Championing culturally responsive leadership for evaluation practice. In P. M. Collins & R. Hopson (Eds.), *Building a new generation of culturally responsive evaluators through AEA's Graduate Education Diversity Internship program. New Directions for Evaluation, 143*, 37–47.

3

Championing Culturally Responsive Leadership for Evaluation Practice

Lisa Aponte-Soto, Deborah S. Ling Grant, Frances Carter-Johnson, Soria E. Colomer, Johnavae E. Campbell, Karen G. Anderson

Abstract

The Graduate Education Diversity Internship (GEDI) program empowers students of color to become adaptive leaders, change agents, partners, and facilitators through exposure to theory, experiential training, leadership development, and mentorship in order to advance culturally responsive evaluation (CRE) practices that respond to context and community values in a respectful and positive manner (Nelson-Barber, LaFrance, Trumbull, & Aburto, 2005). A case study of the first six GEDI cohorts was conducted to evaluate the program's impact on CRE leadership development. This chapter validates how GEDI transformative leadership strategies can be applied by any profession to champion CRE practitioners and promote a society that values social justice, equity, and democratic change. © Wiley Periodicals, Inc., and the American Evaluation Association.

The authors of this chapter are among the nine members of Evolution, the sixth cohort of the AEA GEDI program.

Disclaimers: This work was prepared while Lisa Aponte-Soto was a doctoral student at the University of Illinois at Chicago. The opinions expressed in this article are the author's own and do not reflect the view of the OMG Center for Collaborative Learning or the New Connections Program.

This work was prepared while Frances Carter-Johnson was a postdoctoral associate at the Massachusetts Institute of Technology. The opinions expressed in this article are the author's own and do not reflect the view of the National Institutes of Health, the Department of Health and Human Services, or the United States government.

Introduction

The United States is becoming increasingly culturally diverse, but much work remains to prepare evaluators to respond to communities that differ from their cultural contexts. These needs are best addressed by recruiting, developing, and retaining a diverse workforce (Vappie & Sontag, 2003). The AEA GEDI program for students of color serves as a pipeline to promote culturally responsive evaluation (CRE) capacity building across various practice disciplines. The program's investment in CRE talent development is reflected through technical skill development and team building in both research and evaluation. More notably, the program empowers students to move beyond applied research and evaluation to become adaptive, service-oriented, transformational leaders of CRE practices. As change agents, GEDI alumni adopt a social justice approach of democratic leadership to build the capacity of the evaluation profession to work in racially, ethnically, and culturally diverse settings. Findings from qualitative data inform leadership qualities and competencies essential for promoting CRE practices. Evaluators and students of color will benefit from CRE guiding principles and implications for effecting social change in diverse service communities.

Literature Review

Training culturally responsive evaluators with varied disciplinary- and population-specific expertise is a well-documented need (Chaplin, Hopson, & Stokes, 2011; Manswell-Butty, Reid, & LaPoint, 2004; Mertens & Hopson, 2006; Nelson-Barber et al., 2005). The literature suggests that ignoring issues, such as the impact of variability within subgroups and the multiplicity, fluidity, and nonneutrality of culture, can lead to misinterpretation of evaluation outcomes and ineffective interventions and policies when evaluators are not culturally responsive to or natives of the communities with which they work (Kirkhart, 2010). A historical limit in the number of evaluators from specific underrepresented racial, ethnic, and cultural communities guided development of the AEA GEDI program and its grounding in concepts of CRE, leadership development, and training of new evaluators. CRE is well described in the evaluation literature as well as in this issue and therefore is presented in this section in a limited fashion to simply remind the readers of the foundational concepts (Hood, 2000; Lee, 2007; Manswell-Butty et al., 2004). Three main CRE components of culture, context, and responsiveness were foundational to the GEDI program's goals and evaluation training to avoid using a traditional deficit-based model that leans on mainstream benchmarks normalized on the majority by being deliberately inclusive and respectful of the stakeholders at the margins (Hopson, 2009).

Aligned with the literature that supports leadership development and training as necessary for developing core competencies to increase knowledge and skills (Charan, Drotter, & Noel, 2001; Doyle & Smith, 2001; Fried & Johnson, 2001), the GEDI program's goal is to build and manage talent with an integral premise of training students of color to become agents of change and leaders of CRE. The traineeship promotes personal transformation and supports the growth of critical capacities to ensure the sustainability of the students' agency (Burke, 2002) as evolving champions and leaders of CRE.

The extant literature on training programs for increasing the pool of evaluators of color with research backgrounds or degrees emphasizes competency in research design, quantitative and qualitative analytical methods, and statistics or technical training (Manswell-Butty et al., 2004; Smith, 2011). While such training is important for the technical aspects of evaluation, there is often minimal encouragement in practice for evaluators to pay conscious attention to their value judgments, their cultural contexts, and/or the background of the population of interest when designing or leading the evaluation. Similarly, there is limited research encouraging leadership development in training new evaluators (Manswell-Butty et al., 2004). The few studies providing evidence of leadership development models comparable to the GEDI program only address short-term, broad, and programmatic outcomes, such as implementation in one setting. These studies do not provide core leadership competencies applicable in a variety of programmatic and organizational settings. Thus, additional research is needed to identify core leadership competencies and illustrate the benefits of implementing these in evaluation traineeships while maintaining consciousness of existing cultural lenses. The GEDI program provides a unique opportunity to inductively uncover leadership competencies through the varied experiences of participants.

Methodology

A collective case study of the first six cohorts was conducted by the 2009–2010 cohort to capture participant perspectives on how the program training fostered adaptive leadership through the employment of CRE strategies that substantively and politically address complex issues of culture in evaluation practice. A sample of 32 former GEDI participants provided responses for the study. Semistructured interviews were conducted in person or by phone between fall 2009 and spring 2010. In summer 2011, additional qualitative survey data were collected from a convenience sample of seven members of the sixth cohort using a structured seven-item protocol. Interview questions probed the degree to which participants valued specific program components and engaged in CRE practices as a result of their GEDI experience. The protocol explored CRE leadership practice by inquiring whether participants have transformed their own, others', or organizational evaluation strategies as a result of their involvement in GEDI. Interview data also facilitated evaluation of GEDI program improvement strategies.

NEW DIRECTIONS FOR EVALUATION • DOI: 10.1002/ev

Using HyperRESEARCH, a qualitative data analysis application, an inductive approach was applied to extract key points and experiences. Interview transcripts were reviewed using open and axial coding processes (Corbin & Strauss, 2008) to respectively determine dominant themes, and identify specific examples illustrating each theme. Transcripts were read individually and then collectively analyzed by question. The goal was to identify the narrative of each specific case before comparing narratives across all transcripts (Chase, 2005).

Results

This section cites the experiences GEDI alumni considered critical to their leadership development as service-oriented, culturally responsive evaluators. GEDIs identified four core leadership competencies for advancing CRE: (a) knowledge and skill development, (b) confidence and empowerment, (c) ownership and commitment, and (d) sociopolitical acumen. Implications are discussed for mobilizing CRE through community engagement, increased dialogue, interdisciplinary partnerships, and pipeline development for building and sustaining program capacity.

Service Leadership Experiences

Most GEDI interns reported having minimal formal evaluation training prior to the program. Various learning formats expanded their leadership skills including AEA conference workshops, GEDI seminars, and program internships. Team-based activities and relationships with mentors integrating CRE dialogue, conversations, and collaboration helped lay the foundation for participants to take AEA service-oriented leadership positions, support the GEDI program, and implement CRE practices in their own careers. Namely, one intern lectured in a graduate course to promote CRE and another mentored GEDI members at her own site. Working with expert evaluators also motivated GEDIs to serve at AEA events by leading interest groups, serving on committees, and reviewing abstracts for conferences. An alumna from Cohort 6, who was unfamiliar with AEA until becoming a GEDI, shared how she continued to grow professionally because of her involvement with the organization. *I am currently an active member of AEA... I serve as a TIG Co-Chair... I enjoy being a member because it helps me feel connected to the larger context of evaluation and provides opportunities for professional development.* Thus, GEDI interns' leadership capacity grew as a result of their service to the AEA community and beyond.

Core CRE Leadership Competencies

GEDI leadership experiences promoted ownership of evaluation responsibilities, intercommunity collaboration, and abilities to adapt to multicultural contexts to engage in cultural sensitivity and scholarship in

NEW DIRECTIONS FOR EVALUATION • DOI: 10.1002/ev

evaluation. The program afforded participants various learning contexts through their site placement, conference trainings, seminars, and speakers. Respondents identified four core leadership competencies for advancing CRE.

Knowledge and skill development. Technical evaluation training was an integral part of increasing GEDIs' knowledge and skills in cultural competency with a sociohistorical frame. A GEDI from Cohort 6 attested that the program provided *a basic foundation on evaluation practice, CRE practice theory, and skills, tools, and resources for developing, conducting, and reporting evaluations with a culturally responsive lens.*

Participants underscored their increased capacity to apply CRE in multiple cultural contexts that are inclusive of all marginalized groups. A second cohort GEDI elaborated, *I came into the program with an understanding, but it helped to expand my thinking beyond the African American community... I [also] learned about gender politics and the balance of power.*

Alumni also attributed their credibility and job marketability to the skills gained directly from their internships and the program. A Cohort 6 graduate corroborated, *After participating in GEDI, I have been sought after as an evaluator by organizations in need of evaluation at universities and foundations. In sum, not only do I feel more credible as an evaluator after GEDI but others also recognize this increased credibility and potential to be a leader in evaluation.* A member of Cohort 5 added, *The technical skills that I learned that I didn't have before [were] a definite benefit. I wouldn't have been as marketable without [them].*

As part of CRE leadership development, GEDIs felt mobilized to be change agents, challenge the status quo, and lead cultural competency efforts. One Cohort 6 alumnus reflected, *The program has enhanced my critical and proactive thinking skills and has helped mold me into a change agent to advocate for, lead, and manage CRE projects.*

Confidence and empowerment. Interactions with influential evaluation mentors and thought leaders in CRE practices enabled GEDIs to have greater confidence as leaders and to support and give voice to vulnerable groups and populations. An alumnus from Cohort 3 shared, *People on the board of AEA [who] have influenced evaluation for decades [are] telling you, 'you are the future of evaluation.'* Participants also felt self-assured after exchanging experiences with other graduate students of color. A Cohort 1 graduate recalled, *I had never been in an academic setting with persons of color, it increased my confidence.*

In addition, shared experiences and knowledge of democratic principles empowered GEDIs to become leaders in the field. A GEDI from the sixth cohort affirmed, *The experience in GEDI helped me to establish an understanding of sound evaluation practices... [and gave me the confidence to lead] ... and empower others to [practice] evaluation. I was able to share with colleagues and mentees how I approach evaluation from a culturally responsive perspective.*

Ownership and commitment. GEDIs described a mutual respect and trust with mentors that enhanced their dedication to the program. The program leadership's level of investment and general concern for their career success further strengthened the GEDI's sense of ownership and commitment. One participant from the third cohort noted, *Dr. Hopson was very committed. He invested in all of us individually. He was concerned about your career, life and school … To have somebody totally committed to you as a student and as a professional, made you more committed—a reciprocal respect and relationship was established.*

GEDIs also exemplified their ownership and commitment to the program by being actively engaged in AEA efforts including serving and leading on AEA committees, presenting scholarly work, recruiting future participants, collaborating across cohorts, and facilitating GEDI coordinator and participant selection. A member of the fifth cohort substantiated that *cohorts and ties between cohorts and leadership, and opportunities to serve in or at AEA in some sort of capacity are ways that show commitment and [support] culturally responsive evaluation.*

Sociopolitical acumen. Respondents drew upon the social and political capital imparted by the GEDI program to become culturally responsive evaluators and researchers, which in turn positioned them to embrace and engage in CRE efforts and to expand on as well as spearhead new networks postgraduation in support of CRE practices (e.g., collaborating with other AEA GEDI cohorts and influential evaluation leaders, and launching new Topical Interest Groups in AEA). Alumni tapped into peers, mentors, program coordinators, AEA leaders, and seasoned evaluators to help provide them with the collective skills and power to serve as transformative CRE change agents. A fourth cohort GEDI shared the value of these meaningful interactions: *The face-to-face connections with CRE champions and attending AEA sessions on CRE influenced me to become an advocate.* GEDIs also expressed the benefits of mentoring and coaching gained from interacting with professionals in the field. A Cohort 6 member reported, *The program chairs, sponsors, and mentors have taught me how to navigate difficult situations from negotiating contracts to asserting myself and voicing human rights for my benefit as well as others.*

Implications for Championing CRE Practices

GEDIs gained a greater understanding for championing CRE through the program training coupled with their lived experiences as individuals of color. Among the notable best practices, GEDIs recognized the importance of engaging community stakeholders at every step of the evaluation process to avoid making assumptions that may lead to problematic results (e.g., language discordance) and ensure that services are suitable, aligned, and tailored to specific community needs. A Cohort 6 GEDI highlighted the value of being inclusive of patients as well as community health workers as key *informants to help develop and evaluate programs regarding patient incentives, health worker access, and program acceptability to improve health outcomes.* Recognizing the underrepresentation of evaluators of color, program graduates also emphasized the demand for building CRE capacity through feeder programs like GEDI by recruiting and training bright interns of color, sustaining the cadre of culturally responsive evaluators, and encouraging them to serve as CRE advocates and champions. A Cohort 2 graduate suggested a formalized GEDI alumni network *to maintain cohesiveness as family and establish relationships within the pipeline across cohorts and [extend] mentoring that way.* In addition to practitioners of color, GEDIs urged increased cross-cultural dialogue and interdisciplinary partnerships with practitioners from across the many fields represented in the evaluation community to promote knowledge and awareness of the benefits of and strategies for applying CRE. Another member of Cohort 2 recalled her efforts to elicit dialogue on CRE in and outside the classroom setting: *Any time you ... open that dialogue, that's impactful! I include it even in the most unlikely dialogue [when I teach my students and ... in discussions about organizational] growth and development.*

However, GEDIs advise that the dialogue may fall short without sustainable practices to expand the GEDI program and appropriate support systems that incorporate an honest discourse on managing real-world constraints encountered when attempting to practice evaluation in a culturally responsive way. For example, GEDI alumni reported facing obstacles conveying the importance of CRE practices as well as implementing these at internship settings or places of employment. As a solution, program graduates proposed that these objectives may be achieved by building the pipeline of students of color and providing meaningful internship experiences that prepare transformative leaders for institutional and policy changes.

Discussion

Burke (2002) describes leadership as the most influential component to catalyze organizational change and foster a sustainable culture. As emerging transformational leaders, GEDI alumni hold the capacity to influence others to spur efforts including "a change mission, strategy and culture" (Burke, 2002, p. 16). Professional development activities imparted through the GEDI program honed student leadership qualities including knowledge and skill building, teamwork, and service leadership.

GEDI interns' CRE capacity was increased through the knowledge and skills acquired from participating in evaluation projects that prepared them to work with different populations and cultures. For example, knowing and understanding historical perspectives and the evolution of CRE practices were salient to the talent and skill development of GEDI members. Having a sense of history facilitates team cohesion and ownership, and promotes leadership (Chaplin et al., 2011). In addition, formal and informal discussions with program staff, mentors, peers, and AEA board members on cultural, sociopolitical, and social justice awareness encouraged confidence and empowerment. GEDI program directors set the stage for a family-oriented community, and these seedlings plus additional relationships that emerged from the GEDI network among cohort members and across cohorts built a sense of community that fostered program pride and commitment to champion CRE. Team building has been regarded as a vital component of success and growth of an organization (Fried & Johnson, 2001). The development of a diverse network of relationships also allows for team members to evolve as leaders (Charan et al., 2001). More importantly, the sociopolitical acumen afforded through the GEDI network of alumni and leadership made interns more marketable and competitive for higher positions of leadership across evaluation career paths. A supportive environment builds confidence and is crucial to the career success of students of color (Thomas, 2001).

GEDIs also identified four core leadership competencies for advancing CRE practices that contributed to their ability to serve as CRE change agents. When encountered by resistance for practically applying CRE and/or gaining support from their internship sponsors or clients for implementing CRE practices, GEDIs leveraged their program experiences and leadership competencies to overcome challenges to serve as CRE leaders and advocates for diversity-driven evaluation efforts. Service leadership exemplified by alumni and influential mentors led to volunteerism at AEA activities, such as leading TIGs and conducting presentations on CRE practices both formally and informally at AEA-sponsored events. GEDI also served on AEA committees, reviewed abstracts for AEA conferences, and peer-mentored incoming GEDI scholars. Service to the greater evaluation community also extended to increasing the knowledge base and communication of CRE practices beyond AEA by guest lecturing at universities and presenting at local conferences to promote CRE, and mentoring junior GEDI members.

Additionally, GEDIs uncovered implications for mobilizing leaders of color to diffuse CRE. Specifically, program graduates acknowledged that suitable evaluation methodology includes partnering with the community to tailor data collection instruments. This makes findings more meaningful and avoids misleading interpretations (Hopson, 2009; Manswell-Butty et al., 2004). Alumni also advocated for building the GEDI pipeline to meet the needs of trained CRE practitioners of color as well as increasing CRE dialogue to promote and foster cross-cultural partnerships to serve communities of color.

Although evaluation education is a key program component, ultimately the function of democratic, transformative leadership gained through professional development, and experiential service to others commanded the mobilization of GEDIs as CRE champions by cultivating leaders of color adept to humbly navigate and serve diverse communities to address their toughest problems (Chaplin et al., 2011). The ability to cultivate adaptability has been characterized as being instrumental for leadership development (Dye & Garman, 2006). Therefore, it is necessary to recognize that while knowledge and skill development are critical to laying the foundation of leadership development, the deployment of CRE "...is not [simply] a matter of technique or skill, but ultimately [extends beyond this to] ... leadership and adaptation" (Chaplin et al., 2011, p. 8).

Conclusions

Cultural competency is not about mastering a skill set or a one size fits all prescriptive; it is a lifelong process of self-reflection, self-awareness, and self-critique (Hunt, 2005). Therefore, responsiveness requires evaluators to practice cultural humility by being reflective and understanding of their own cultural values, adapting to each unique community, and tailoring methodology at each step of the way to establish new ways of thinking that are inclusive of all cultures. The AEA Statement on Cultural Competence supports the role of cultural competence in evaluation theory and practice as "critical for the profession and for the greater good of society" (American Evaluation Association, 2011, p. 4). Thus, CRE promotes social justice and human rights and can have major impact, as a GEDI alumna from the sixth cohort states, *I now feel that I have the skill set, though evolving, to critically reflect on the context of cultural relevance, and to serve as a transformative advocate of CRE practice, particularly in the healthcare field where CRE can literally save lives.*

To champion CRE practices, it is imperative to build a pipeline of CRE practitioners, particularly evaluators of color, to bridge communication gaps between organizations and communities being served. The GEDI program develops leadership and evaluation skills in new evaluators of color to support and sustain their evaluation practice with a culturally responsive lens and lead these efforts in marginalized communities (Chaplin et al., 2011). Cultivating core leadership competencies helps mobilize new evaluators of color to be agents of change both as individuals and in the greater evaluation community.

GEDI interns are evolving as CRE champions by fostering cross-cultural partnerships and practices and adapting to challenges faced in mobilizing CRE practices. GEDIs emphasized that CRE calls for inclusivity of not only interdisciplinary practitioners of color prepared to lead social justice efforts, but also a diverse mix of evaluators (e.g., representative of cultural diversity as well as different disciplines in the field) through dialogue and deliberation. As a third cohort GEDI states, it is important to equally maintain relationships with empathetic CRE practitioners, while engaging in and embracing dialogue with people who hold diverse perspectives *to broaden the concept of what it is to be culturally responsive, as it is not limited to working with marginalized populations.*

References

American Evaluation Association. (2011). *American Evaluation Association public statement on cultural competence in evaluation.* Retrieved from http://www.eval.org /p/cm/ld/fid=92

Burke, W. W. (2002). *Organization change: Theory and practice.* Thousand Oaks, CA: Sage.

Chaplin, S., Hopson, R. K., & Stokes, H. (2011). *Making leadership happen: Theory and practice for social justice in a pipeline program* (Unpublished manuscript). Pittsburgh, PA.

Charan, R., Drotter, S., & Noel, J. (2001). *The leadership pipeline: How to build the leadership powered company.* San Francisco, CA: Jossey-Bass.

Chase, S. E. (2005). Narrative inquiry: Multiple lenses, approaches, voices. In N. K. Denzin & Y. S. Lincoln (Eds.), *The SAGE handbook of qualitative methods* (3rd ed., pp. 651–679). Thousand Oaks, CA: Sage.

Corbin, J., & Strauss, A. L. (2008). *Basics of qualitative research: Grounded theory procedures and techniques* (3rd ed.). Thousand Oaks, CA: Sage.

Doyle, M. E., & Smith, M. K. (2001). Classical leadership. *The encyclopedia of informal education.* Retrieved from http://www.infed.org/leadership/traditional_leadership.htm

Dye, C. F., & Garman, A. N. (2006). *Exceptional leadership: Sixteen critical competencies for healthcare executives.* Chicago, IL: Health Administration Press.

Fried, B. J., & Johnson, J. A. (2001). *Human resources in healthcare: Managing for success.* Washington, DC: AUPHA Press.

Hood, S. (2000). Commentary on deliberative democratic evaluation. In K. E. Ryan & L. DeStefano (Eds.), *New Directions for Evaluation: No. 85. Evaluation as a democratic process: Promoting inclusion, dialogue, and deliberation* (pp. 77–83). San Francisco, CA: Jossey-Bass. doi:10.1002/ev.1163

Hopson, R. K. (2009). Reclaiming knowledge at the margins: Culturally responsive evaluation in the current evaluation moment. In K. E. Ryan & J. B. Cousins (Eds.), *The SAGE international handbook of educational evaluation* (pp. 429–446). Thousand Oaks, CA: Sage.

Hunt, L. M. (2005). Beyond cultural competence: Applying humility in clinical settings. In N. M. P. King, R. P. Strauss, L. R. Churchill, S. E. Estroff, G. E. Henderson, & J. Oberlander (Eds.), *The social medicine reader: Vol. 2. Social and cultural contributions to health, difference, and inequality* (2nd ed., pp. 133–137). Durham, NC: Duke University Press.

Kirkhart, K. E. (2010). Eyes on the prize: Multicultural validity and evaluation theory. *American Journal of Evaluation, 31,* 400–413.

Lee, K. (2007). *The importance of culture in evaluation: A practical guide for evaluators.* Retrieved from Colorado Trust website: http://www.coloradotrust.org /attachments/0000/2208/CrossCulturalGuide.r3.pdf

Manswell-Butty, J. L., Reid, M. D., & LaPoint, V. (2004). A culturally responsive evaluation approach applied to the talent development school-to-career intervention program. In V. G. Thomas & F. I. Stevens (Eds.), *New Directions for Evaluation: No. 101. Co-constructing a contextually responsive evaluation framework: The talent development model of school reform* (pp. 37–47). San Francisco, CA: Jossey-Bass. doi:10.1002/ev.105

Mertens, D., & Hopson, R. K. (2006). Advancing evaluation of STEM efforts through attention to diversity and culture. In D. Huffman & F. Lawrenz (Eds.), *New Directions for Evaluation: No. 109. Critical issues in STEM evaluation* (pp. 35–51). San Francisco, CA: Jossey-Bass. doi:10.1002/ev.177

Nelson-Barber, S., LaFrance, J., Trumbull, E., & Aburto, S. (2005). Promoting culturally reliable and valid evaluation practice. In S. Hood, R. K. Hopson, & H. T. Frierson (Eds.), *The role of culture and cultural context: A mandate for inclusion, the discovery of truth, and understanding in evaluative theory and practice* (pp. 59–85). Greenwich, CT: Information Age.

Smith, D. A. (2011). Making the case for the humanities in evaluation training. In S. Mathison (Ed.), *New Directions for Evaluation: No. 131. Really new directions in evaluation: Young evaluators' perspectives* (pp. 15–20). San Francisco, CA: Jossey-Bass. doi:10.1002/ev.372

Thomas, D. A. (2001). The truth about mentoring minorities: Race matters. *Harvard Business Review, 79*, 99–107.

Vappie, K., & Sontag, L. (2003). When mentoring makes a difference. *Bridges, 9*, 1–6.

LISA APONTE-SOTO *is the National Deputy Director of the Robert Wood Johnson Foundation New Connections Program at the OMG Center for Collaborative Learning.*

DEBORAH S. LING GRANT *is an adjunct researcher in public health with the RAND Corporation.*

FRANCES CARTER-JOHNSON *is an AAAS Science and Technology Policy Fellow at the National Institutes of Health's Center for Scientific Review.*

SORIA E. COLOMER *is an assistant professor in the College of Education at the University of South Florida.*

JOHNAVAE E. CAMPBELL *is a senior evaluation specialist with Evaluation, Assessment, and Policy Connections at the University of North Carolina's School of Education in Chapel Hill.*

KAREN G. ANDERSON *is the CQI and evaluation coordinator at Families First; she is also the creator of the DIY Evaluation blog, On Top of the Box Evaluation.*

Gómez, R. L., Ali, A., & Casillas, W. (2014). Mentorship and the professional development of culturally responsive evaluators in the American Evaluation Association's Graduate Education Diversity Internship (GEDI) program. In P. M. Collins & R. Hopson (Eds.), *Building a new generation of culturally responsive evaluators through AEA's Graduate Education Diversity Internship program*. New Directions for Evaluation, 143, 49–66.

4

Mentorship and the Professional Development of Culturally Responsive Evaluators in the American Evaluation Association's Graduate Education Diversity Internship (GEDI) Program

Ricardo L. Gómez, Asma Ali, Wanda Casillas

Abstract

In this study, we used Q methodology to investigate perspectives on mentorship among alumni of the Graduate Education Diversity Internship (GEDI) program. We asked participants to think retrospectively and give their opinion on the most important characteristics a GEDI mentor should have, based on what they would have liked or needed when they participated in the GEDI program. Three different perspectives on mentoring emerged from participants. They show that mentoring is not unidimensional; that perceptions and expectations of mentoring are defined to a great extent by the professional needs, background, and expectation of the participants. We suggest that the program takes those needs and expectations into consideration and use them as criteria for selecting mentors. © Wiley Periodicals, Inc., and the American Evaluation Association.

Program

The American Evaluation Association Graduate Education Diversity Internship (GEDI) program is currently in its 10th cycle and has 62 alumni and

---

The authors of this chapter participated in Legacy, the fifth cohort of the AEA GEDI program.

NEW DIRECTIONS FOR EVALUATION, no. 143, Fall 2014 © 2014 Wiley Periodicals, Inc., and the American Evaluation Association. Published online in Wiley Online Library (wileyonlinelibrary.com) • DOI: 10.1002/ev.20093 alumnae. Mentorship is a core feature of the GEDI program, which is advanced and utilized as a distinctively interpersonal form of learning. During the GEDI program, formal and informal mentorship of the interns is combined with professional development workshops, participation in conferences, and hands-on evaluation experience through practical evaluation projects to introduce students to the evaluation profession. After participants complete the internship, formal mentorship relationships developed during the program are encouraged to continue as a part of the alumni experience. Though all components of the program work in concert, mentorship and networking are essential to the GEDI program experience.

In this study, we sought to understand perspectives on mentorship among alumni of the GEDI program. Particularly, the current study focuses on what participants think should be the most important characteristics of a GEDI mentor.

This study is based on the premise that mentoring is a powerful personal and professional development tool—one that is multidimensional and can serve different purposes. Thus, we expect to contribute to the evolution of the GEDI program by tapping into the experience of former participants and channeling their opinions into an explanation of what sort of mentorship would have been most relevant to them based on their experience, career goals, and professional aspirations.

The authors used Q methodology (Brown, 1980; Stephenson, 1953) as the main tool for inquiry. Q is an established methodology used to investigate people's subjectivity—i.e., opinions, beliefs, or attitudes about an issue. Participants were asked to sort a set of statements that characterize mentorship relationships. Then, participants' rankings were analyzed using correlation and by-person factor analysis (Stephenson, 1953), resulting in three distinct factors interpreted to better understand the mentorship experiences of the GEDI interns. The factors are discussed with implications for the continued mentorship of future GEDI generations.

Background

Existing literature cites numerous benefits of mentorship to early career participants—known as protégés—in these relationships (Chao, Walz, & Gardner, 1992; Scandura, 1992; Whitely, Dougherty, & Dreher, 1992). Professional articles on the role of mentorship on professional development abound across several academic literatures, including higher education, health professions, and teaching. These articles often include conceptual models of the mentorship program, including the structure of formal mentorship programs, or suggest requirements for informal mentorship programs related to specific careers or interests. More recent studies point to positive outcomes for early career mentees compared to their peers who do not participate in mentoring relationships.

New Directions for Evaluation • DOI: 10.1002/ev

Definitions of Mentorship

The traditional definition of mentorship describes a "relationship between a younger adult and an older, more experienced adult [who] helps the younger individual learn to navigate the adult world and the world of work" (Kram, 1985, p. 2). The study of mentoring relationships is often traced to the seminal work by Levinson, Darrow, Klein, Levinson, and McKee (1978) on the career development of adult men. In their work, Levinson and colleagues describe the relationship that develops with a mentor as one of the most important experiences of early career and young adulthood.

Mentors reportedly are not only a source of learning for protégés, but they also play a key role in the development of protégés' self-esteem and work identity (Dalton, Thompson, & Price, 1977; Kanter, 1977; Shapiro, Haseltine, & Rowe, 1978). These studies point to positive career outcomes for the protégés who are engaged in mentor relationships. Later work by Kram (1985) points to two tracks of mentorship outcomes associated with this relationship: (a) formal knowledge and skill building, and (b) psychosocial development. In recent years, emerging literatures have differentiated between two distinct types of psychosocial career outcomes associated with mentorship. The primary outcomes include easily measurable components such as salary and promotions, while secondary career outcomes include career satisfaction and professional networking opportunities. A wide variety of mentorship models have been advanced across several professions, with the greatest numbers of models being advanced in the management, health professions, and education literatures (Bozeman & Feeney, 2007). Typically, in these literatures, mentorship models align with one of the two tracks noted above or a combination of elements from the two. Additionally, different levels of importance emerge for the various components of the mentor–protégé relationship (Allen & Eby, 2004) on the continuum between knowledge and skill development and psychosocial components of mentoring. Allen and Eby (2004) suggest further study to establish the importance of the primary (salary and career outcomes) versus secondary psychosocial outcomes (job satisfaction and career opportunities) across different disciplines in order to establish key characteristics of mentor–protégé relationships.

For the purposes of this study, we adopted the following definition of mentoring initially proposed by Bozeman and Feeney (2007):

> ...a process for the informal transmission of knowledge, social capital, and psychosocial support perceived by the recipient as relevant to work, career, or professional development; mentoring entails informal communication, usually face-to-face and during a sustained period of time, between a person who is perceived to have greater relevant knowledge, wisdom, or experience (the mentor) and a person who is perceived to have less (the protégé). (p. 731)

NEW DIRECTIONS FOR EVALUATION • DOI: 10.1002/ev

From this perspective, mentorship involves the transfer of knowledge, skills, and social capital related to the workplace from the mentor to the protégé. The GEDI program provided opportunities for the participants to build knowledge about evaluation and culturally responsive evaluation as well as social networking and informal opportunities to develop social capital and networks within the evaluation profession. As such, this project addresses all three expectations of the mentor–protégé relationship in order to address which ones emerge as the most important to early career GEDI alumni.

Mentorship Models

Mentorship programs may be classified into four general categories of mentor–protégé relationships, including (a) apprenticeship models, (b) training program models, (c) coaching models, and (d) collegial models (Allen & Eby, 2004; Davis, 2005). These models differ in the prescribed relationship between mentor and protégé, as well as their individual emphases on skill building, networking, or emotional support components of the mentor–protégé relationship. Two of the models, the apprenticeship model and the training program model, are related to the development of the protégés' professional knowledge or skills. In these models, the mentor serves as a guide for the enhancement and development of expected knowledge within the profession often as a direct or ancillary supervisor to the mentee. The coaching model and the collegial model of mentorship are focused on the development of psychosocial components of the profession. Several forms of mentorship opportunities are included and encouraged in the GEDI experience, including formally required mentorship during the course of the program and access to a larger professional network within the American Evaluation Association after graduation from the program.

The first model, the *apprenticeship model* of mentoring, is often utilized in established and regulated training programs for early career professionals. These apprenticeship models of mentorship are common among early career physicians and attorneys. In these types of programs, early career protégés work alongside a "seasoned" mentor in order to develop their professional skills and networks. A distinguishing factor of these types of programs is that the mentor is often the protégé's assigned supervisor and often a gatekeeper into the profession through formal evaluations of the protégé. However, these formalized programs, while guiding the protégé in formal skill and knowledge training, may not adequately support the emotional or social needs of the protégé.

A second model, the *training program* model, combines semiformal, unregulated mentorship with a structured training program. The training program model involves a formal pairing of a protégé with a mentor who performs the job duties of the protégé's profession, but is not responsible for evaluating the protégé's job performance (Davis, 2005). In addition,

NEW DIRECTIONS FOR EVALUATION • DOI: 10.1002/ev

the training program model often provides structured interactions for selection and maintenance of the mentor–protégé relationship. Examples of this model of mentorship include adult teacher training programs, or urban school leadership residencies, where protégés are paired with nonsupervising teachers or principals while completing an extended internship in their field. The training program model provides protégés access to additional knowledge and support in their chosen field, while providing the confidentiality needed to garner the emotional and social support of the mentor. The GEDI program provides students with an opportunity to interact with seasoned professionals and scholars, who assist them in developing evaluation protocols and other skill building to benefit their program site.

Another variation of mentoring is seen in *coaching models*, where program mentors support the protégé through both their program experience and in their subsequent professional career. This model combines formalized training with unstructured opportunities to access experienced practitioners in the field. These programs provide resources for the protégé outside of their typical work environment by promoting access to cross-functional or cross-institutional relationships with senior leaders in the profession. Such relationships provide protégés with additional perspectives about their knowledge or skill development, as well as their role within profession (Davis, 2005; Kram & Isabella, 1985). A U.S. Department of Labor Study in 1999 found that the classroom learning followed by coaching mentorship leads to better learning outcomes than traditional classroom learning alone (Benabou & Benabou, 1999). The GEDI program provides this type of access to evaluation mentors through its requirement of selecting mentors in the field. These mentors inform GEDI participants' evaluation work throughout the program.

Finally, *collegial mentorships* are informally structured relationships with mentors often initiated by the protégés themselves. Collegial mentorship reflects the earliest forms of workplace mentorship, before mentorship became a component of formalized training programs for professional development. In these relationships, informal workplace relationships provided psychosocial or networking support for the protégé in relationships often described as "friendships" (Davis, 2005).

Typically, training or workplace programs have capitalized on the benefits of these relationships by providing access to a network of supporters and/or alumni who serve as mentors for early career professionals. Protégés seeking these types of mentorship relationships report less interest in technical skill building or knowledge. Instead, the mentors serve as sounding boards, provide emotional support, and promote access to wider collegial networks for the protégé. After graduation, the GEDI program provides this support for its alumni through programming at the AEA Annual Meeting, alumni events, and continued informal interactions with mentors.

Professional mentorship can occur through established professional training programs or education programming. In each model of mentorship, the structural formality of the mentor and protégé relationship as well as the nature of the relationship itself plays a central role in its perceived benefits to the protégé (Davis, 2005). While early research on mentorship (Kram & Isabella, 1985) indicated that mentorship that fulfills the most functions would be most beneficial to protégés, recent research indicates that different types of mentorship may be beneficial for different protégés or at different points within the protégés' careers.

Early career evaluators may possess any combination of expectations from their mentor–protégé relationship. This study will explore expectations of the mentorship relationship and mentors among participants in the GEDI program. Building from the established models of mentorship, this research will inform the mentorship expectations and models that would be most useful to diverse, early career evaluators who participated in the GEDI program.

Method

The researchers used Q methodology (Brown, 1980; McKeown & Thomas, 1988; Stephenson, 1953) to investigate GEDI participants' views about mentoring. At its most basic description, in a typical Q study, participants express their opinion by ranking a set of stimuli—statements, pictures, objects, etc. During this process, participants place the items along a continuum, usually from "Most Agree" to "Most Disagree," or a similar configuration that allows them to sort the items in some kind of rank order.

The final rankings (known as the Q sorts) are then correlated and factor analyzed. This process helps to identify Q sorts that share a similar structure and therefore represent a similar perspective or point of view.

It has been widely used in fields such as political science, nursing, education, and marketing, and recently, sparked the interest of the evaluation community. For instance, the American Evaluation Association has seen an increase in Q methodology-related submissions (e.g., Balutski, Janson, & Militello, 2013; Brown, Militello, Balutski, & Janson, 2013; Gomez, 2012; Gomez & Shartrand, 2011; Shartrand, Gomez, & Giordan, 2009).

Q method differs from other approaches for investigating people's opinions (surveys, focus groups, interviews) in that individuals assess the importance of statements relative to other statements. This allows them to focus on the issues that are most important to them and, thus, the perspectives that emerge from the data are more likely to be those of the participants of the study than those of a researcher imposing predefined categories on participants.

Procedure

The procedure for Q methodology research consists of definition of topic and selection of statements, selection of participants, ranking of statements, and statistical analysis and interpretation. Each of these steps is explained below.

Definition of Topic and Selection of Statements

For this study we searched for statements about the purpose of mentoring relationships in higher education literature. We collected an initial bank of 72 statements—called the Q concourse (Brown, 1980; Stephenson, 1953). After revising and rewriting the statements and checking for duplication, we finally settled for a list of 28 statements. In Q methodology, the final list of statements to be sorted by the participants is called the Q sample (Table 4.1).

Selection of Participants

For this study, participants were recruited with the help of the current administrators of the GEDI program, who provided us with contact information of 59 alumni of the program. Participants were contacted via email. Twelve email addresses had expired and could not be used. In total, 26 individuals responded to the invitation to participate. They had been selected to participate in the GEDI program between 2003 and 2012. The group was comprised of 15 females and 11 males, with experience as evaluators ranging from zero to seven years at the time of participating in the study. Other demographic information including race, ethnicity, current employer, and highest degree achieved at the time of participation in the study is shown in Table 4.2.

Data Collection: Q Sorting

The study was conducted online using FlashQ, an open-source application for performing Q sort research (Hackert & Braehler, 2007). Participants were sent a link via email to access the statements. Participants were asked to read through the 28 statements and then to sort them into three piles using the following condition of instruction: "In your opinion, what should be the most important characteristics of a GEDI mentor?" The underlying motive behind this instruction was to motivate participants to think back to their GEDI experience and rank the statements in terms of what they needed or would have preferred as interns. They were not evaluating or ranking their mentorship experience during their participation in the program; we were just trying to gauge their opinion of what characteristics, in their view, make a good mentor.

In one pile participants placed those statements about which they felt *positive* and in the other pile those statements about which they felt *negative*. If there were statements toward which the participants felt neutral, they were instructed to place them in a middle *neutral* pile. This provisional sorting process was then followed by the final Q sort, which began with

Table 4.1. Q Sample Used in the Study

No.	*In your opinion, what should be the most important characteristics of a GEDI mentor? A mentor ....*
1	who meets with me regularly.
2	who listens to me and understands what I want to achieve as an evaluator.
3	who gives me assignments or tasks that prepare me for an evaluation position after graduation/participation in GEDI.
4	who helps me to lay out concrete steps to achieve success in my career as evaluator.
5	who challenges me intellectually.
6	who exposes me to new evaluation ideas and experiences.
7	who gives me assignments that present opportunities to learn new skills.
8	who provides me with positive feedback regarding my performance as evaluator.
9	who encourages me to prepare for advancement in my evaluation career.
10	who discusses my questions or concerns regarding feelings of competence, commitment to advancement, or relationships with colleagues.
11	who encourages me to try new ways of behaving in my role as evaluator.
12	who encourages me to talk openly about anxieties and fears that detract from my work.
13	who helps me to expand my professional networks.
14	who introduces me to influential people in the evaluation field.
15	who has experience mentoring other evaluators.
16	who invites me collaborate in her evaluation projects.
17	who invites me to coauthor journal papers or books.
18	who gives advice without dictating actions.
19	who shares history of his/her career with me.
20	who demonstrates good listening skills in our conversations.
21	who shares personal experiences as an alternative perspective to my problems.
22	who keeps feelings and doubts I share with him/her in strict confidence.
23	who shares my same attitudes and values regarding evaluation.
24	I would like to be like my mentor when I reach a similar position in my career.
25	who is a recognized individual in the evaluation field.
26	with an active research and publication agenda.
27	who is an active member of professional evaluation societies.
28	with strong technical and analytical skills.

participants looking at the statements in the *positive* pile and allocating them a place in the right-hand side of the sorting grid (Figure 4.1).

Allocating items to the ranking grid forces participants to sort the statements relative to each other and reveal their actual preferences (Webler, Danielson, & Tuler, 2009). In some cases, the number of statements in an initial pile exceeds the number of places available in the sorting grid. For example, there can be more statements in the positive pile than spaces in the grid. In this case, participants have to make compromises in what statements they choose to allocate to the available spaces in the sorting grid.

NEW DIRECTIONS FOR EVALUATION • DOI: 10.1002/ev

Table 4.2. Demographics of Participants

Category	Options	N = 26
Years of evaluation experience	No evaluation experience	9
	1 year	5
	2 years	3
	3 years	4
	4 years	1
	5 years	2
	6 years	1
	7 years	1
Employer	Federal Government	2
	Independent	1
	NGO	8
	Other	3
	State Government	1
	University	11
Area of experience	Elementary/secondary education	3
	Higher education	2
	Public Health	9
	Sciences and Engineering (STEM)	5
	Other/unspecified	7
Race	American Indian or Alaska Native	4
	Asian	1
	Black/African American	16
	Mixed (self-defined)	5
Ethnicity	Hispanic	3
	Non-Hispanic	23
Gender	Female	15
	Male	11
Highest degree completed	Master's	18
	Doctoral	8

The participants repeated the same process with the *negative* and the *neutral* pile. When participants were finished, they had sorted the 28 statements into the shape shown in Figure 4.1. At the end of the sorting procedure, participants had the opportunity to write down and explain why they ranked the statements in the way they did. Their open-ended responses were used in the interpretation of the findings.

Statistical Analysis

Statistical analyses in Q methodology seek to find patterns across participants' Q sorts. This is done by identifying how alike (or unlike) each participant's Q sort is from that of other participant. To this end, the researcher first looks for intercorrelations among participants' N Q sorts (i.e., persons, not traits, statements, or items are correlated); then these intercorrelations are confirmed by carrying a by-person factor analysis on the $N \times N$ correlation matrix (Hurtienne & Kaufmann, 2011). The resulting factors are composed

NEW DIRECTIONS FOR EVALUATION • DOI: 10.1002/ev

Figure 4.1. Q-sorting distribution used in the study ($n = 28$).

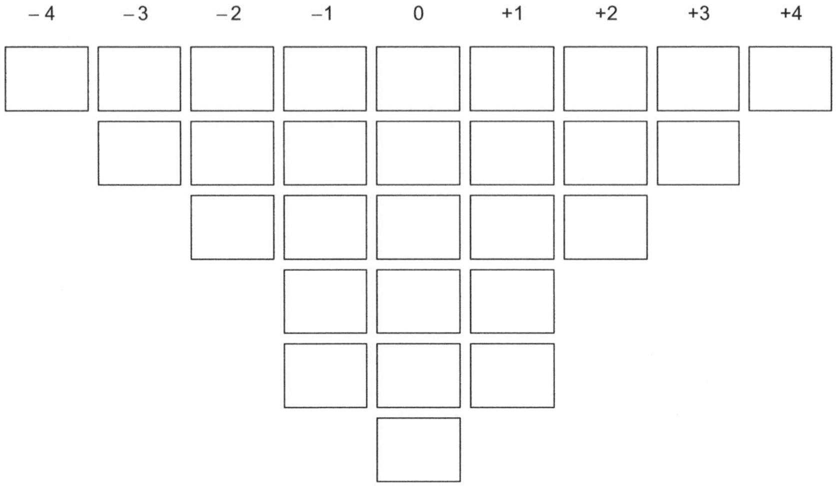

| −4 | −3 | −2 | −1 | 0 | +1 | +2 | +3 | +4 |

by the participants whose Q sorts have a similar structure, are related to each other, and therefore indicative of a shared perspective or opinion. For this study, the analysis was conducted using PQMethod (Schmolck, 2012), a dedicated computer software for the analysis of Q sort data. To analyze the data, a correlation matrix was created to compare levels of agreement among the 26 Q sorts followed by a factor analysis on the correlation matrix to group together, as one factor, Q sorts that had similar rankings.

Results

Three distinct factors or perspectives were extracted from the analysis. The final three factors accounted for 23 of the 26 completed Q sorts. Three sorts that did not meet the significance criteria in any of the factors were eliminated from the analysis.

Interpretation and Discussion

For the interpretation of factors, we follow the approach proposed by Watts and Stenner (2012). We created interpretation crib sheets for each one of the factors. We identified, for each factor, the items given the highest ranking, the lowest ranking, and the items ranked higher or lower than by any other study factors. In the section that follows, we present the interpretation of each perspective with its accompanying interpretation crib sheet.

Perspective A: I Want to Be a Professional Evaluator and Need Mentors Who Help Me to Achieve That. This perspective is shared by persons who seem to be considering professional or academic careers in

Table 4.3. Interpretation Crib Sheet for Factor 1

No.	*Statement and Ranking in Factor Array*
	Item ranked at +4
04	A mentor who helps me to lay out concrete steps to achieve success in my career as evaluator. +4
	Items ranked higher by factor 1 than by any other factor
03	A mentor who gives me assignments or tasks that prepare me for an evaluation position after graduation/participation in GEDI. +3
14	A mentor who introduces me to influential people in the evaluation. +3
13	A mentor who helps me to expand my professional networks. +2
17	I would like to have a mentor who invites me to coauthor journal papers or books. +2
	Items ranked lower by factor 1 than by any other factor
05	Mentor who challenges me intellectually. +1
10	A mentor who discusses my questions or concerns regarding feelings of competence, commitment to advancement, or relationships with colleagues. −1
20	A mentor who demonstrates good listening skills in our conversations. −1
22	A mentor who keeps feelings and doubts I share with him/her in strict confidence. −1
11	A mentor who encourages me to try new ways of behaving in my role as evaluator. −3
	Item ranked −4
23	I would like to work with a mentor who shares my same attitudes and values regarding evaluation. −4

evaluation (Table 4.3). Therefore, central to this perspective are mentors who can help them acquire marketable skills through specific tasks or assignments that prepare them for an evaluation position after graduation or participation in the GEDI program [3, +3].[1] As one participant stated when explaining their sorting decisions,

> More than anything, the process of becoming an evaluator requires apprenticeship in actually conducting evaluations. Conducting evaluations are the assignments/opportunities that would make the GEDI experience transformative; it is experience with a capacity-building purpose. In order for GEDI to truly 'learn by doing,' mentors should consider encouraging the cultivation and integration of new skills in GEDI assignments.

Combined with the importance of gaining practical skills through tasks and assignments is an emphasis on the importance of mentors who invite them to coauthor journal papers or books [17, +2]. This might indicate that people who share this perspective are considering careers in higher education.

Participants who share this perspective see networking as a very important element in the path to becoming successful evaluators. This perspective strongly expresses the expectation that mentors help interns connect them to influential people in the evaluation community [14, +3] and expand their professional networks [13, +2]. As one of the participants who loaded into this factor expressed:

> Networking is highly important if an individual seeks to broaden their perspective and scope in the field of evaluation. Social networks are also highly influential to the success of individual if they present you with access to other systems and stakeholders.

On the other side of the spectrum, for participants who loaded into this factor, mentors and protégés sharing the same values and attitudes about evaluation is the least important aspect of a mentoring relationship [23, −4]. Furthermore, the development of a personal connection with the mentor is not central to the goals of a mentoring relationship [20, −1; 22, −1]. As one of the participants commented:

> [...] as long as there is a space of mutual professional respect between mentor and protégé, I don't think personal issues are warranted or appropriate topics of conversation. That stated, I feel that all mentors have the professional know-how to engage with protégés in personal dialogue without coming across as dismissive or uninterested.

Or as other participant expressed,

> This is least important because it is something you can get from your academic advisor or any other friend or professional and not as important in the grand scope of what I really would like to get from a GEDI mentor.

Perspective B: I Would Like to Have a Mentor Who Can Show Me How to Wear the Evaluation Hat When the Opportunity Arises. This perspective places primary emphasis on the development of new skills. Individuals who share this opinion prefer mentors who provide them with opportunities to learn new skills (Table 4.4).

(7, +4). What they seek in a mentor is someone with strong technical and analytical skills (28, +3), who challenges them intellectually (5, +3), who provides them with positive feedback regarding their performance as evaluators (8, +2), and who meets with them regularly (1, +2).

They do not expect that a mentor helps them to achieve success in career as professional evaluators (17, 0). In fact, for this perspective, publishing and expanding their professional networks are not important characteristics that define mentoring relationships (17, −3). Therefore, this is likely to be the perspective of individuals who are not necessarily interested in pursuing academic or full-time professional careers in evaluation. Rather, they seem to be more interested in being able to use or apply their evaluation skills in their workplace or when the opportunity arises. This perspective

Table 4.4. Interpretation Crib Sheet for Factor 2

No.	Statement and Ranking in Factor Array

Item ranked at +4

07   A mentor who gives me assignments that present opportunities to learn new skills. +4

Items ranked higher by factor 1 than by any other factor

05   Mentor who challenges me intellectually. +3

28   A mentor with strong technical and analytical skills. +3

01   A mentor/mentor who meets with me regularly. +2

08   A mentor who provides me with positive feedback regarding my performance as evaluator. +2

Items ranked lower by factor 1 than by any other factor

13   A mentor who helps me to expand my professional networks. −1

16   A mentor who invites me to collaborate in her evaluation projects. −1

21   A mentor who shares personal experiences as an alternative perspective to my problems. −3

17   I would like to have a mentor who invites me to coauthor journal papers or books. −3

26   A mentor with an active research and publication agenda. −3

Item ranked −4

25   I would like to have a mentor who is a recognized individual in the evaluation field. −4

is summarized by a participant reflecting about the role of mentoring in the GEDI program:

> [GEDI] mentoring experience should prepare me to think about the different hats I could wear as an evaluator and to develop those that fit me best—and to see where the opportunities were! Also, it helps when you're feeling like a ship at sea applying for jobs.

Perspective C: I Need a Mentor Who Is a Good Listener and I Can Reach Out to for Advice. For this perspective, the most important characteristic of a mentor is their capacity to listen actively [2, +4; 20, +3] and give advice [18,+1] when needed (Table 4.5).

They do not expect a mentor to have strong technical and analytical skills (28, −1), or who is a member of professional evaluation societies (27, −3), but someone to whom they can go to when they have questions or doubts. Different from the previous perspectives, they do not think it is important to have a mentor who gives them assignments or feedback on their performance as evaluator (8, −2). As stated by one of the participants whose Q sort loaded significantly on this factor, "I am not looking for more work to do, but refinement and assistance with what is already on my plate and situation myself for the future that I envision." This perspective seems to be aligned with the *collegial mentorship* approach (Davis,

Table 4.5. Interpretation Crib Sheet for Factor 3

No.	Statement and Ranking in Factor Array
	Item ranked at +4
02	Mentor who listens to me and understands what I want to achieve as an evaluator. +4
	Items ranked higher by factor 1 than by any other factor
20	A mentor who demonstrates good listening skills in our conversations. +3
22	A mentor who keeps feelings and doubts I share with him/her in strict confidence. +2
18	A mentor who gives advice without dictating actions. +1
19	A mentor who shares history of his/her career with me. +1
	Items ranked lower by factor 1 than by any other factor
6	A mentor who exposes me to new evaluation ideas and experiences. +1
7	A mentor who gives me assignments that present opportunities to learn new skills. +1
3	A mentor who gives me assignments or tasks that prepare me for an evaluation position after graduation/participation in GEDI. 0
28	A mentor with strong technical and analytical skills. −1
	Item ranked −4
23	I would like to work with a mentor who shares my same attitudes and values regarding evaluation. −4

2005), in which protégés give priority to mentors who serve as sounding boards, provide emotional support, and help them to access wider collegial networks.

Interestingly, participants who loaded into this factor are those who reported longer evaluation experience. Thus, it is likely that this perspective on mentoring stems from their experience as evaluators. The median experience time as evaluators in this group was 6 years, ranging from 3 to 6 years. This might explain that they see mentors not as teachers who can teach them new skills, but as confidants who they can trust with questions, feelings, and doubts (22, +2). Technical skills, as one participant observed, "can be acquired from training or independent study."

Similar to Factor A, Factor C also rejects the idea that mentors and mentees should share the same attitudes and values regarding evaluation [23, −4]. In fact, one of the participants sees this as detrimental for the professional development of evaluators:

> Working with a mentor who shares your values and attitudes with regard to evaluation is not always good because then a mentee does not acquire an alternative viewpoint. I've been mentored from professionals who I haven't agreed with and our differing perspectives actually enriched the relationship and the mentoring experience.

Conclusion

This study set out to investigate perspectives about mentoring among former participants of the GEDI program. Specifically, we wanted to know what characteristics they considered more important in a mentoring relationship. We asked participants to think retrospectively and give their opinion on the most important characteristics a GEDI mentor should have based on what they would have liked or needed when they participated in the GEDI program.

The results of this study highlight the characteristics of mentoring relationship desired by early career evaluators. Whether mentoring relationships have been established through formal or informal aspects of the GEDI program, early career GEDI clearly desire specific outcomes from these relationships, based on their professional aspirations and tenure in the field. Three distinct perspectives about mentoring emerged from the analysis.

The first perspective (I want to be a professional evaluator and need mentors who help me to achieve that) is held by a group of evaluators who are likely considering professional or academic careers in evaluation. What they seek in a mentor is somebody who helps them to develop technical skills, expands their professional networks, and invites them to collaborate in their research and writing projects. In this group, participants seek to develop the skills, connections, and professional profile that make them marketable in the professional or academic evaluation sector.

A second perspective (I would like to have a mentor who can show me how to wear the evaluation hat when the opportunity arises) emerges from a group of individuals who are not necessarily interested in pursuing professional or academic careers in evaluation. They seem to be primarily interested in developing a set of skills that allows them to be informed users of evaluation when the opportunity arises. Therefore, for them, the most beneficial mentoring relationship is one which involves a mentor with strong technical and analytical skills, who challenges them intellectually, and who provides relevant feedback regarding their performance as evaluators. Different from the first perspective above, for participants who share this perspective, coauthoring journals or books, or collaborating with mentors in evaluation projects are not the most important outcomes of mentorship.

The third perspective (I need a mentor who is a good listener and I can reach out to for advice) emerged from a group of participants who came into the GEDI program with a fair amount of knowledge and experience. They are confident they have, or can develop, the skills they need to be successful evaluators. Therefore, what they seek in the program is an advisor, a person they can reach out to for advice or for answers to their questions. For this perspective, skill-based training was less important than the ability to "confirm doubts" and "gain clarity" about their existing projects.

As training program for evaluation, the GEDI program provides many opportunities for participants and alumni to connect with potential

NEW DIRECTIONS FOR EVALUATION • DOI: 10.1002/ev

mentors. GEDI participants and interns obtain access to mentors through many different types of mentor–protégé relationship models. The findings from this study show that mentoring is not unidimensional; that perceptions and expectations of mentoring are defined to a great extent by the professional needs, background, and expectation of the participants. Our results reinforce the continued, and even expanded, use of both the formal and informal mentorship relationships. On the one hand, very early career GEDI participants expect formal introduction to professional expectations. However, a few years into their careers as evaluators, GEDI members desire more informal and equal relationships with informal mentors. Thus, the formal aspects of mentoring should not be considered a substitute for informal mentoring relationships but should be offered as a complement or an addition to informal mentoring.

In addition, the selection of informal mentors through the development of the career seems particularly important for GEDI participants. Thus, the fact that the GEDI program involves the mentor and protégé in the formation of the mentoring partnership seems to be particularly relevant. When mentors and protégés perceive they have a voice in the matching process, they may invest more in the relationship.

This is an exploratory study and the findings cannot be generalized. That is not the intended use of Q methodology. There is still much to be understood about mentorship and the early career evaluator. However, mentoring is an important professional development tool that can be used to enlarge the extent and impact of the GEDI program.

One of the recommendations that we make based on our findings is that the GEDI program identifies career plans and aspirations of participants during the selection process and uses those as criteria for selecting mentors. Much can be learned and gained by associating with people who have the skills, expertise, and willingness to help early career evaluators achieve their individual professional goals. It is not unreasonable to assume that mentoring relationships in which mentors and protégés share similar perspectives about mentoring and career paths are likely to be more productive, meaningful, and relevant for the protégé. This study also opens up more avenues for investigation. Further research on this issue can include surveying the current mentors and protégés for their information about how mentoring impacted their career plans. Also, since the GEDI program requires the selection of formal and informal mentors, comparative studies with nonmentored early career evaluators may provide additional insights into the impact and effectiveness of mentoring programs.

Since the early 1970s, many books and articles have been written about mentoring across several disciplines and fields. However, much remains to be uncovered about the mentorship of evaluators. We began this research with the idea that we each had different requirements and expectations from the mentorship relationship. As the GEDI program matures and alumni become further established in their careers, the requirements will almost certainly advance. Pursuing research about mentorship outcomes and other mentorship needs should enhance theoretical and practical understandings of mentorship needs and results for evaluators throughout their career cycle.

Note

1. The first number corresponds to the statement in the merged Q sort and the second one to its ranking.

References

Allen, T. D., & Eby, L. T. (2004). Factors related to mentor reports of mentoring functions provided: Gender and relational characteristics. *Sex Role, 50*(1–2), 129–139.

Balutski, B., Janson, C., & Militello, M. (2013, October). *What Q can do for you*. Paper presented at the annual meeting of the American Evaluation Association, Washington, DC.

Benabou, C., & Benabou, R. (1999). Establishing a formal mentoring program for organizational success. *National Productivity Review, 18*(2), 1–8.

Bozeman, B., & Feeney, M. K. (2007). Toward a useful theory of mentoring: A conceptual analysis and critique. *Administration & Society, 39*(6), 719–739.

Brown, S. (1980). *Political subjectivity: Applications of Q method in political science*. New Haven, CT: Yale University Press.

Brown, S., Militello, M., Balutski, N., & Janson, C. (2013, October). *Q methodology: A participatory evaluation approach that quantifies subjectivity*. Workshop held at the annual meeting of the American Evaluation Association, Washington, DC. Retrieved from http://www.eval.org/e/in/eid=1&s=66&print=1&req=info

Chao, G. T., Walz, P. M., & Gardner, P. D. (1992). Formal and informal mentorship: A comparison on mentoring functions and contrast with nonmentored counterparts. *Personnel Psychology, 45*, 619–636.

Dalton, G. W., Thompson, P. H., & Price, R. L. (1977). The four stages of professional careers—A new look at performance by professionals. *Organizational Dynamics, 6*(1), 19–42.

Davis, A. L. (2005). *An investigation of formal mentoring relationships and programs: A meta-analysis* (Doctoral dissertation). City University of New York, New York.

Gomez, R. (2012, October). *Opinions count . . . so get them right: Using Q methodology to inform program evaluation and planning*. Paper presented at the annual meeting of the American Evaluation Association, Minneapolis, MN.

Gomez, R., & Shartrand, A. (2011, November). *Beyond 'agree' and 'somewhat disagree': Using Q methodology to reveal values and opinions of evaluation participants*. Paper presented at the annual meeting of the American Evaluation Association, Anaheim, CA.

Hackert, C., & Braehler, G. (2007). FlashQ (Version 1) [Computer software]. Retrieved from http://www.hackert.biz/flashq/downloads/

Hurtienne, T., & Kaufmann, G. (2011). Methodological biases. Inglehart's world value survey and Q methodology. *Journal of Human Subjectivity, 9*(2), 41–69.

Kanter, R. M. (1977). *Men and women of the corporation*. New York, NY: Basic Books.

Kram, K. (1985). *Mentoring at work: Developmental relationships in organizational life*. Lanham, MD: University Press of America.

Kram, K., & Isabella, L. A. (1985). Mentoring alternatives: The role of peer relationships in career development. *Academy of Management Journal, 28*(1), 110–132.

Levinson, D. J., Darrow, C. N., Klein, E. B., Levinson, M. H., & McKee, B. (1978). *The seasons of a man's life*. New York, NY: Alfred A. Knopf.

McKeown, B., & Thomas, D. (1988). *Q methodology*. New York, NY: Sage.

Scandura, T. A. (1992). Mentorship and career mobility: An empirical investigation. *Journal of Organizational Behavior, 13*, 169–174.

Schmolck, P. (2012). *PQMethod* [Computer Software], Version 2.1.3. Retrieved from http://schmolck.userweb.mwn.de/qmethod/

Shapiro, E. C., Haseltine, F. P., & Rowe, M. P. (1978). Moving up: Role models, mentors and the patron system. *Sloan Management Review, 19*(3), 51–58.

Shartrand, A., Gomez, R., & Giordan, J. (2009, November). *The chemistry of innovation: An exploratory assessment of attitudes toward innovation among academic chemists.* Poster presented at the annual meeting of the American Evaluation Association, Orlando, FL.

Stephenson, W. (1953). *The study of behaviour: Q technique and its methodology.* Chicago, IL: University of Chicago Press.

Watts, S., & Stenner, P. (2012). *Doing Q methodological research: Theory, method and interpretation.* London, UK: Sage.

Webler, T., Danielson, S., & Tuler, S. (2009). *Using Q method to reveal social perspectives in environmental research.* Greenfield, MA: Social and Environmental Research Institute.

Whitely, W., Dougherty, T. W., & Dreher, G. F. (1992). Correlates of career-oriented mentoring for early career managers and professionals. *Journal of Organizational Behavior, 13*, 141–154.

RICARDO L. GÓMEZ *is an assistant professor of quantitative research and evaluation methods in the College of Education at Universidad de Antioquia, Medellín, Colombia.*

ASMA ALI *has an MA in sociology and is currently ABD in urban planning and policy, with a concentration in Community/Economic Development at the University of Illinois at Chicago College of Urban Planning and Policy.*

WANDA CASILLAS *is currently a research fellow with the University of Michigan Rackham Graduate School and program evaluation consultant with a PhD from the Department of Human Development at Cornell University.*

NEW DIRECTIONS FOR EVALUATION • DOI: 10.1002/ev

Bryan, M. L., & O'Sullivan, R. (2014). Shaping a new generation of culturally responsive
evaluators: Program director perspectives on the role of the internship experience. In P. M.
Collins & R. Hopson (Eds.), *Building a new generation of culturally responsive evaluators
through AEA's Graduate Education Diversity Internship program. New Directions for Evaluation, 143*, 67–81.

Shaping a New Generation of Culturally Responsive Evaluators: Program Director Perspectives on the Role of the Internship Experience

Michelle L. Bryan, Rita O'Sullivan

Abstract

*In this chapter, we reflect on the role of the internship experience (also known as
the practical evaluation project placement) within the overall design and function of the Graduate Education Diversity Internship (GEDI) program as well as
its relationship to program goals and outcomes. We argue that explicit consideration of the program's cultural context is critical for understanding the impact
of the internship experience on the program's overall quality and effectiveness.
Drawing on our experiences as former codirectors, as well as our former interns'
reflections, we address the ways in which cultural and contextual factors within
their internship sites, and within the larger program itself, affected the interns'
ability to incorporate tenets of culturally responsive evaluation into their internship experience. Framing the internship as both a pedagogical and a practical
space for merging evaluation theory and practice, we discuss our attempts to
understand its role in supporting interns' evolving understanding of culturally
responsive evaluation. © Wiley Periodicals, Inc., and the American Evaluation Association.*

A cknowledging a pressing need for the evaluation community to increase its number of evaluators of color (and evaluators from other underrepresented groups), to stimulate reflexive conversations regarding Culturally Responsive Evaluation (CRE), and to strengthen its capacity for working effectively across racially, ethnically, and culturally diverse settings, the American Evaluation Association (AEA) has sponsored, supported, and championed the Graduate Education Diversity Internship (GEDI) program for the last 10 years. One of the program's four core components, the internship experience has played a critical role in the program administration's efforts to achieve program goals. Given the fundamental role of the internship within the program's framework, as well as the direct and indirect relationships of the internship to the program's outcomes, this chapter focuses on a number of contextual factors that have a significant impact on the overall internship experience.[1]

Specifically, we believe ensuring the GEDI program's continued success (and that of programs like it) depends on developing a better understanding of how contextual factors related to (a) program norms and traditions, (b) the organizations and agencies sponsoring interns, and (c) how the evaluation projects on which interns work may combine to influence the extent to which the internship experience provides students with an opportunity to put their evolving understanding of CRE into practice. Our reflections on the role and function of the internship experience, as well as feedback solicited from former interns with whom we worked, were guided by the following question: *In what ways do the practical evaluation experiences obtained during their internship placement enhance interns' abilities to engage in CRE?*

Within the framework of this issue, we seek to contribute to a more nuanced understanding of the curricular structures that guide the GEDI program by focusing on the internship experience. Importantly, we advance a frame for theorizing about the internship experience as well as our reflections on its development. In particular, those who are developing programs to strengthen the pipeline into the field of evaluation or programs that include an internship experience as a critical component of a program's design may find value and utility in the "lessons learned" documented here.

The authors remind the reader that the reflections shared in this chapter should be understood within the context of the two academic years (2009–2011) during which we served as codirectors of the GEDI program. We acknowledge the likelihood that a number of the contextual challenges we reference around the internship component may have since been resolved by subsequent directors.

The Internship Experience

The National Association of Colleges and Employers (NACE) defines an internship as:

NEW DIRECTIONS FOR EVALUATION • DOI: 10.1002/ev

a form of experiential learning that integrates knowledge and theory learned in the classroom with practical application and skills development in a professional setting. Internships give students the opportunity to gain valuable applied experience and make connections in professional fields they are considering for career paths; and give employers the opportunity to guide and evaluate talent. (NACE, 2011, para. 4)

The value and benefits of participating in an internship experience have been well documented. As Carlson and Halbrooks (2003) point out, the enduring appeal of internship stems from the mutual benefits accrued by both the intern and the organization for which they work. They explain that for employers, "internships provide a workplace and training ground for a 'source' of highly motivated technicians and pre-professionals who want to work and learn more" (p. 4). For interns, "internships provide an opportunity to explore career opportunities with potential 'full-time' employers, learn new skills, gain needed work experience for professional certifications, begin to develop a network of professional colleagues, enhance their professional resume, and pursue their future dreams" (p. 5).

Importantly, the robust nature of research on internship programs has led to the development and documentation of several "best practices." Since 2002, NACE has listed the following directive as its top best practice:

> Providing interns with real work is number one to ensuring your program's success. Interns should be doing work related to their major, that is challenging, that is recognized by the organization as valuable, and that fills the entire work term. (NACE, 2012, para.1)

The GEDI program internship experience (along with intensive mentoring, professional networking, and expert lectures) serves as a foundational component of the GEDI program. Specifically, the internship experience is directly tied to the goal of ensuring that a student's participation in the program significantly increases the likelihood of their choosing a career in evaluation or finding ways to incorporate evaluation into their disciplinary area(s) of expertise. Either outcome fulfills the AEA's commitment to creating a pipeline into the profession, thus enhancing the larger field of evaluation through strengthening our capacity as a profession to work across diverse settings.

During our time as program directors, we worked with 17 graduate students who interned at nine sponsor agencies (e.g., universities, nonprofits, foundations, government agencies, research and evaluation firms, etc.) near their graduate institutions. The majority of their internship experiences afforded the interns an opportunity to engage multiple aspects of the evaluation process while working on either a single or multiple evaluation projects, depending on each organization's needs. For roughly nine months, students spent the equivalent of two days per week immersed

New Directions for Evaluation • DOI: 10.1002/ev

in experiential learning, attempting to integrate the knowledge and theory they were learning through the GEDI program curriculum with the practical application and skills development facilitated within the organizational and evaluation cultures at their internship site.

Situating the Internship: A Core Component of the Curricular Framework

A significant number of introductory evaluation courses taught in U.S. colleges and universities begin with an overview of the field, followed by several days on its historical roots and relevant forebearers. The focus then shifts to the core components in the "evaluation process" with extended discussions of key tools used in that process (e.g., needs assessments, logic models, data collection protocols, etc.). The rest of the semester is then spent exploring how that process gets taken up through various theoretical, conceptual, and methodological approaches to evaluation practice. Within this curricular framework, if/when CRE is addressed it is often situated as one of these approaches.

In contrast, the GEDI program's curriculum begins by positioning evaluation as a "situated practice" (Arzubiaga, Artiles, King, & Harris-Murri, 2008), reflecting the cultural backgrounds, experiences, and ways of knowing of each and every individual connected to a program, regardless of their role or position. Such positioning facilitates a foundational understanding of evaluation as being intimately and irrevocably *tied to culture*. Bolstered by this understanding, the curriculum seeks to cultivate dispositions and knowledge bases necessary for working to "develop the conceptual and practical skill set necessary to effectively interpret educational, social, behavioral, and organizational initiatives, programs, and policies that are implemented in a variety of culturally diverse settings and with culturally diverse groups" (Christie & Vo, 2011, p. 549).

Within the larger curricular framework of the program, the internship serves as the experiential mechanism for the practical application of interns' efforts to merge their existing research expertise with the knowledge they acquire about evaluation theory and practice via the GEDI program curriculum (e.g., readings, expert lectures, workshops, projects, assignments, etc.). Indeed, it is primarily through the internship experience that efforts to extend the interns' research capacities to evaluation are actualized. Given the centrality of cultural competence and responsiveness to the program's curriculum, the internship experience serves as the vehicle through which interns come to applied understandings regarding the necessity for conducting evaluations that are culturally responsive as well as the role of cultural competence within that process. Given this emphasis, students inevitably arrive at their internship sites with their cultural lenses heightened. They bring to their internship experience expectations (both conscious and unconscious) that their sites will serve as both a pedagogical and a practical space for merging (culturally responsive) evaluation theory and practice. In essence, they begin their internships eager to see what CRE looks like in practice.

Situating the Internship: Logistics and Limitations

When we began our directorship of the GEDI program in the early summer of 2009, the program had been operating for five years. Consequently, during our first year we committed to maintaining the program's structural integrity, refraining from making any substantial changes. While we had significant or complete control of several aspects of the program (e.g., selection of interns, curriculum development, selecting of trainings location, etc.), in other areas, our actions were guided by a number of program norms, organizational processes, and standing practices that had shaped its culture. The first organizational process we encountered was the selection of internship sites, as the AEA had predetermined six of the nine internship sites for the 2009–2010 academic year.

Given the logistical, diplomatic, and economic challenges that can accompany any program's efforts to find agencies willing to sponsor internships, we were grateful to have a majority of sites already in place. Importantly, our lack of understanding of the historical context that shaped the selection of these organizations led us to assume that their selection had been tied to a commitment not only to the program in general but also to its explicit goal of developing culturally competent evaluators. Thus, with CRE-committed organizations (we assumed) at the ready, we began reviewing program applications attempting to seek alignment between an organization's needs, an applicant's disciplinary background, and geographic proximity between organizations and applicants. However, we quickly found ourselves struggling to make suitable matches as the background and interests of our top candidates rarely aligned with the opportunities available at (and the specific evaluation needs of) the preselected sponsor agencies. Ultimately, our commitment to accepting the top candidates resulted in some students interning with organizations whose work was *outside* a student's disciplinary home as those organizations were in closest proximity to the student's graduate institution.

Moreover, we carried our assumption about sponsor agencies' commitment to CRE into our efforts to identify the remaining internship sites. Yet we quickly discovered that contextual factors (including the relative cost of sponsoring an intern, the number of interns we desired to accept into the program, and the impact of the recent economic downturn) meant that it was neither practical nor plausible for us to require that sponsor agencies express an interest in or commitment to understanding, valuing, or engaging in CRE. Thus, while our efforts resulted in the selection of organizations whose needs more closely matched our top candidates' disciplinary backgrounds, we did so uncertain as to the organizations'

NEW DIRECTIONS FOR EVALUATION • DOI: 10.1002/ev

appreciation for and levels of awareness, knowledge, and application of CRE. In light of the challenges we experienced during the selection of organizations and intern–organization matching processes, we accepted that the quality and effectiveness of the students' internship experiences that year would be varied.

Theorizing the Internship Experience

Guided by previous program norms, we drafted *Memorandums of Agreement* (examples of which had been shared with us by the previous administration) between the GEDI program, the sponsor agencies, and the interns. However, while the memoranda contained expectations for what interns would accomplish during their time with the organization, there were no stated expectations or outcomes for the internship experience to which sponsor agencies were held accountable. Consequently, as the students began reporting back to us about their internship experiences, we discovered that while internship supervisors were required to be experienced evaluators, and were aware that developing cultural competence and understanding CRE were prominent features of the GEDI program, there was no expectation that they craft an internship experience rich in opportunities for interns to merge the theoretical and practical tenets that undergird CRE, nor that interns engage in evaluations that served racially, ethnically, or other culturally diverse populations. Further, given the caliber of the organizations where several interns had been placed, program norms dictated that the direction of the internship experience be left to the discretion of the internship supervisor. Our understanding that our reach as directors stopped at the organization's front door meant that the extent to which notions and practices related to CRE became a part of a student's internship experience was largely determined by contextual factors within the sponsor organizations.

Accepting the fact that there would be certain program outcomes (some explicit and others implicit) tied to the internship experience over which we had no control, we began theorizing about the intended purpose of the internship experience, its role within the overall framework of the program, and the potential for sponsor sites to serve as spaces for merging theory and practice. As the year unfolded, we listened closely and carefully as the interns talked about the connections (or lack thereof) they were making between their internship work and their evolving understanding of cultural competence and cultural responsiveness in evaluation practice. At our winter seminar, we collaborated with the interns for the development of an emergent framework, grounded in their experiences (as well as our own), to facilitate our efforts to understand the connection between their internship experiences and their evolving understanding of CRE.

Informed by four and a half months of field-based evaluation experience, the interns identified both personal and contextual factors, as well as competing values within their internship sites, that influenced their ability to translate theories, concepts, methodologies, and techniques associated with CRE into practice. Their contributions helped us flesh out important nuances around the three predominant contextual factors identified: the evaluator/intern's experiences and orientations, the client/sponsor agency's organizational context, and the nature of the evaluation task(s) in which one engages. In many ways, the framing reflects what we believe are the experiences of any evaluator (novice to expert) committed to CRE practice. In essence, these three factors and their complex interactions influence the extent to which an evaluation (or, in this case those aspects of the evaluations on which interns were working) reflects cultural responsiveness. Our understanding of these factors is as follows:

- *Evaluator/intern's experiences and orientations.* This factor involves an individual's level of evaluation experience and level of cultural competence within specific settings, as well as their knowledge of and commitment to culturally relevant evaluation practices.
- *Client/sponsor agency's organizational context.* The second factor speaks to the organizational knowledge, understanding, and appreciation of CRE (including how culture is defined within the organization and the extent to which it is valued) held by the agencies who sponsor GEDI interns; the level of cultural awareness and competence held by their staff; and, importantly, their perceptions regarding the relevance of culture to the evaluation (i.e., the extent to which the programs being evaluated have *identifiable* characteristics that reflect their definition of culture, such as targeting marginalized communities, etc.). Importantly, these contextual considerations should be taken into account not only with respect to the sponsor agency but also to programs on whose behalf the agency conducts evaluation.
- *Nature of the evaluation task/internship assignment.* This factor speaks to the extent to which a particular stage of the evaluation process, or specific evaluation task in which the evaluator/intern is engaged, possesses *identifiable* characteristics that lend themselves to culturally informed considerations and responsive practices. For example, interns who were asked to conduct interviews with preexisting protocols or to assist with quantitative data summarizing found few opportunities to apply CRE principles.

Notably, each of these aspects exists within a complex web of contextual factors that bear on the evaluation process including organizational cultures, evaluation resource constraints, temporal constraints, external constraints, and the disciplinary backgrounds that inform stakeholders' and evaluation staff members' epistemological views.

Intern Reflections

In November 2012, we surveyed the 17 former interns from the 2009 and 2010 cohorts in an effort to probe the integrity of the framework. Specifically, we asked them to reflect on their internship experiences during the program and on the extent to which they were ultimately able to use those experiences to enhance their ability to engage in CRE. Focusing on the three factors, we asked them to respond to the following three questions:

1. How, if at all, was your previous evaluation experience an influence?
2. How, if at all, was the culture of the organization in which you were placed an influence?
3. How, if at all, was the nature of your evaluation assignment(s) an influence?

In addition, fully aware that while our framework was useful it did not account for all of the potential influential factors at play, we asked a fourth question:

4. What other factors, if any, do you think influence an evaluator's ability to engage in CRE?

We received responses from 10 of the interns and content analyzed their responses using the framework factors as our analytical categories. We summarize their responses below, including the interns' thoughts regarding additional influential factors.

Prior experiences and orientations. Prior to entering the GEDI program, the interns' limited experiences with evaluation differed markedly, as did their orientations to evaluation. In their responses to this question, the interns addressed their experiences working with different cultural groups and previous evaluation-related experiences that necessitated cultural competence. They also shared how those previous experiences led them to apply to the GEDI program and, in some cases, how those experiences proved valuable during their time in the program and afterward. According to their responses, previous experiences indeed influenced their ability to engage in CRE.

In some cases, CRE became a new construct added to an emerging evaluation practice. As one intern observed, "I had limited previous evaluation experience, so this proved to be an important training and practical opportunity for me and allowed me to learn evaluation from a very important standpoint as a woman of color." Another commented, "Coursework in policy analysis and program evaluation did not mention being culturally responsive as a component to consider when doing such work." Taking a different perspective on the question, one intern responded by positioning her experience in the GEDI program as the "former experience" to which the question referred. Her comments speak directly to the foundation that GEDI program staff seek to develop within students from which they will continue to deepen their understanding and grow their practice:

> I did a process and some outcome evaluation of a water, sanitation, and hygiene education project in Malawi, Eastern Africa, during the summer of 2011. Since I was working in a different country where the language and culture posed challenges, I learned how to be culturally competent in a new environment by continuously engaging with my local counterparts. I worked with them to identify their evaluation needs, best communication and evaluation methods, etc. Together, we created evaluation tools that could be easily understood for low-literate or illiterate participants, developed an evaluation plan that wasn't overly burdensome on the locals, and wrote a report that took cultural factors into consideration.

Client/sponsor agency's organizational culture. Data also supported the sponsor agencies' understanding and appreciation of CRE as contributing to an intern's ability to engage in CRE. Interns responded that an organization's culture, particularly around those aspects we subcategorized as "Mission/Vision/Values," "Ways of Working," and "Orientation to Diversity," informed the ways in which they were able to implement CRE.

Of the three subcategories above, an organization's mission, vision, and values were most often identified as notable influences. For example, one intern wrote:

> My organization was a non-profit aimed at supporting those less fortunate in society. The culture of helping the less fortunate provided a backdrop for and understanding of the principles of culturally responsive evaluation. However, as in most evaluation projects, issues such as time, resources, and a lack of awareness of CRE may have hindered a direct or full application of CRE to the project.

Intern responses also identified organizational practices or "ways of working" that contributed to their ability to engage in CRE:

> One of the greatest organizational strengths was the weekly office meetings. In our weekly discussions about our work, struggles, and client engagements, we were able to openly express our biases or concerns with our projects in a safe environment and, as a team, discuss how to address them. This exposed me to the complexity of evaluation and, when applicable, how to engage in culturally responsive evaluation.

Another intern's reflection demonstrated how an organization's orientation toward diversity was manifest in its organizational practices:

The office's culture influenced my ability to engage in culturally responsive evaluation as a facilitator of multiple projects that dealt with issues in culturally complex organizations. Even though I did not personally work on these projects, the staff meetings and the environment in which I could listen and talk to other research assistants about the evaluations they were working on allowed for me to think about and experience through discussion culturally responsive evaluations in different contexts.

Nature of the evaluation task/internship assignment. The interns' responses indicated that they benefitted when their evaluation tasks allowed them to apply a culturally informed lens. For the interns, those opportunities most often occurred when they were working with or considering the needs and perspectives of diverse clientele, including underserved or marginalized populations. The call to cultural competence also depended on the variety of tasks in which interns were involved, as well as their ability to collaborate with clients and stakeholders. Finally, as one intern suggested, the practices of the programs being evaluated could influence the amount/type of CRE.

The nature of their evaluation assignments within their internship site seemed particularly influential to their ability to engage in CRE. For example, one intern noted:

> My evaluation assignment was the development of an evaluation plan for a system to assess racial equity in non-profit grant-making and work for the organization. The fact that the system was to assess racial equity was my project allowed me to apply a CRE lens in developing the evaluation plan.

Working with culturally diverse groups led another intern to observe:

> My major assignment included conducting phone interviews with college/university stakeholders for a suicide prevention project. I had to interview 4–5 people from each college/university, and one site was located in Guam. Along with interviewing stakeholders across the country and working to quickly build rapport with them on the phone for quality data collection, I was able to learn more about how suicide prevention programs were being implemented at colleges and universities from the perspectives of faculty, counseling staff, administrators, and students.

Additional factors. Though not all interns offered additional factors related to enhancing their abilities to engage in CRE practice, those who did most often mentioned knowledge of self and interpersonal skills. In addressing how personal characteristics and values served as additional factors that contributed to their ability to engage in CRE, one intern spoke of the ways in which her GEDI experience was affirming and validating for her as a young evaluator of color. She noted:

NEW DIRECTIONS FOR EVALUATION • DOI: 10.1002/ev

I believe personal interests/passions/experience is a factor. As a member of a minority group I think it's important that voices of all stakeholders are heard for equity and consideration of a different viewpoint than the decision makers. This is also a personal value . . . one values culturally responsive evaluation and because it is valued they are able to engage in culturally responsive evaluation. In addition to training, education/ coursework as factors, had I not been selected for the GEDI program, I would not have been able to engage in culturally responsive evaluation as an approach.

Finally, according to the interns, embracing CRE also entails learning more about self in relation to culture. In reflecting on her participation in a workshop during her internship, one intern stated:

Other than having strong interpersonal abilities to engage with participants cross-culturally and having the tools to conduct a culturally responsive evaluation, I think it's important to ensure that evaluators have the proper cultural competence training. One of the best cultural competence trainings I attended was "Undoing Racism," which helped me to understand my biases and to be more aware of my prejudices. I also thought it was important to learn how to work with people of different cultures and backgrounds so that I can practice cultural competence in a safe environment, so I volunteered for an inner-city organization for four years.

Implications and Recommendations

We recognize that, for a variety of reasons, an overhaul of the processes by which internship sites are selected is unlikely. However, based on the interns' reflections and our experiences, we believe that the GEDI program's emphasis on CRE could be more fully actualized by intentionally emphasizing that focus in conversations with internship site coordinators, thus positioning sponsor agencies as *critical partners* in achieving the program's goals and objectives. In addition, we suggest that the interns' overall experiences may be enhanced by making explicit both the possibilities and limitations of their internship as a site for integrating theory and practice.

Positioning Sponsor Organizations as Program Partners

Given the commitment of the AEA and of GEDI program administrators (i.e., directors, staff, and program liaison) to strengthen the pipeline of culturally responsive evaluators, it may be beneficial for program leaders to carefully consider the ways in which implicit program outcomes and expectations can be made explicit for sponsor agencies. If two of the primary purposes of the GEDI program are to stimulate reflexive conversations regarding CRE and strengthen the evaluation community's capacity to working effectively with diverse stakeholders across diverse settings, then those purposes should also inform the processes for recruiting and retaining sponsor agencies. In discussing their work with respect to selecting sponsor organizations for their internship, Rodney Hopson (founder of the GEDI program) and Gerri Spilka, codirectors of the Robert Wood Johnson Fellowship program (whose goals are similar to GEDI) shared:

> We have been meeting with the placement agencies, the supervisors and mentors, and inviting them to help us describe what the implications are for culturally appropriate evaluation from the organizational perspective. If organizations are interested in being a part of that conversation, then it will serve as an incentive to participate. (Christie & Vo, 2011, p. 555)

In addition, an initial interest form disseminated to organizations for recruiting purposes might include a section where representatives from potential sponsor agencies are asked to address their organization's mission, vision, and values, and to speak briefly about the organization's beliefs regarding CRE, perhaps beginning with a description of their organization's culture. Including such questions on a recruitment form could serve as a practical way for GEDI program administrators to examine "fit" between sponsor agencies' and GEDI program's goals and objectives, as well as facilitate a critical conversation regarding individual and shared aims.

We believe that such efforts may go a long way toward positioning sponsor agencies as vested program stakeholders. Partnering with organizations that are fully aware of, and who share the program's mission, can strengthen the program in ways that make obtaining the program's goals more likely. Further, as a part of the sponsor agency selection (and/or retention) process, it may be beneficial for GEDI program administrators to share their stance on CRE, as well as the program's theory of change, with organization representatives. Engaging in dialogue around AEA's (2011) statement on cultural competence, for example, could serve as an additional mechanism for exploring fit and seeking common ground. Finally, sharing key aspects of the program's curriculum with sponsor agencies may provide vital contextual information upon which an organization may draw as it considers how to structure an intern's experience and in selecting the program(s) on which an intern might work.

Contextualizing the Internship Experience

We acknowledge that, even if all of the recommendations above are taken up, there is no guarantee that a student's internship experience will be replete with culturally responsive moments and opportunities for growth. Ultimately, then, perhaps the best course of action for program directors is to be open and upfront with interns regarding both the possibilities and limitations of the internship experience. Indeed, through explicitly situating the internship experience within the overall program design and curricular structure, interns' expectations regarding the experience become more fully informed and contextualized by an appreciation for the ways in which program administrators have limited influence on their internship sites.

Nevertheless, were we to revisit the limited role program directors play with respect to internship site experiences, we would caution against increasing their involvement beyond the intentional efforts to collaborate with agencies noted above. We believe that evaluators, both novice and seasoned, who are committed to CRE are likely to experience significant growth in their practice when working in contexts rich with opportunities to engage in culturally responsive practices throughout the evaluation process, as well as in contexts where the relevance, value, and/or utility of such practice may not be readily apparent to colleagues, clients, or other stakeholders. Moreover, while we believe that CRE is steadily gaining momentum among evaluators in training and those currently in the field, our experiences indicate that contemporary evaluators are much more likely to be conducting evaluations in the latter context than in the former.

Importantly, the limitations inherent in the internship experience can be incorporated into the interns' developing understanding of *culture* as a key component of culturally responsive approaches to evaluation. Indeed, notably absent from the intern reflections shared above is an understanding of cultural responsiveness as including the "interrogation of majority culture," as well as an attending to "the cultural location of all evaluation practices" (K. K. Kirkhart, personal communication, September 24, 2013). Consequently, if we were to revisit the program's curriculum, we would be inclined toward revisions that more intentionally emphasized the need for interns to continually deconstruct and reconstruct the meaning and multifaceted nature of culture, perhaps with an eye toward the importance of organizational diversity as emphasized by Collins, Kirkhart, and Brown (Chapter 2 of this issue), with respect to their internship sites.

While we did not fully revisit the curriculum during our tenure, an unintended (though welcome) outcome of engaging our first cohort of interns in the collaborative process of theorizing about their individual and collective experiences was that several of the interns were able to let go of their own anxieties around "not seeing it [culturally responsive evaluation practice]" in their internship sites, or feeling as though they had somehow let us down given their failure to find opportunities "to engage in it." Seeing value in how the framework allowed the interns to place their experiences in context and to gain a better understanding of what was and was not in their control within their site, the framework became a part of the first training session with our second cohort.

Conclusion

As Bertrand Jones notes, "The preparation from the GEDI program provided at the graduate level impacts emerging professionals' ability to conduct sound evaluation and integrate culturally responsive evaluative thought into their evaluation practice" (Chapter 6 of this issue, p. 95). Evaluation data on the GEDI program (Graduate Education Diversity Internship Program, 6th Cohort, 2010) clearly demonstrate that the GEDI program is a powerful mechanism for recruiting, training, and retaining evaluators from diverse backgrounds with strengths in CRE practices into the profession. As one of the four key components of the program, the internship experience significantly contributes to these outcomes.

In this chapter, we have attempted to provide important context for understanding the role of the internship experience within the GEDI program in terms of its contribution to culturally responsive practice and have suggested a framework by which to examine factors that can influence that effectiveness. In sharing this framework and the experiences that contributed to its development, we have attempted to demonstrate the power and potential of the GEDI program, particularly for its participants, even when program administrator's attempts to aligning wants, needs, and commitments sometimes fall short. In light of the program's potential, and the critical role of the internship within its structure, we invite those committed to strengthening the pipeline, particularly those considering the development of similar programs, to continue to think with us about how to best structure internships in ways that maximize the collaborative efforts of programs and their organizational partners.

Note

1. Throughout this chapter, our use of the words "internship" and "internship experience" refers to the component of the program wherein students obtain practical work experience through their placement at a sponsor agency. In other chapters in this issue, this component may be referred to as *practical evaluation project placement*.

References

American Evaluation Association (AEA). (2011). *American Evaluation Association public statement on cultural competence in evaluation*. Fairhaven, MA: Author. Retrieved from http://www.eval.org/p/cm/ld/fid=92

Arzubiaga, A. E., Artiles, A. J., King, K. A., & Harris-Murri, N. (2008). Beyond research on cultural minorities: Challenges and implications of research as situated cultural practice. *Exceptional Children, 74*(3), 309–327.

Carlson, C. R., & Halbrooks, M. C. (2003). *Essential components of a successful internship program*. Westerville: Ohio Nursery & Landscape Association.

Christie, C. A., & Vo, A. T. (2011). Promoting diversity in the field of evaluation: Reflections on the first year of the Robert Wood Johnson Foundation Evaluation Fellowship program. *American Journal of Evaluation, 32*(4), 547–564.

Graduate Education Diversity Internship Program, 6th Cohort. (2010, June). *AEA Graduate Educational Diversity Internship (GEDI) program report*. Paper presented at the American Evaluation Association/Centers for Disease Control Summer Institute, Atlanta, GA.

National Association of Colleges and Employers. (2011). *A position statement on U.S. internships: A definition and criteria to assess opportunities and determine the implications for compensation.* Retrieved from http://www.naceweb.org/about /membership/internship/.
National Association of Colleges and Employers. (2012). *15 best practices for internship programs.* Retrieved from http://www.naceweb.org/recruiting/15_best_practices/

MICHELLE L. BRYAN *is an associate professor of educational foundations and inquiry in the Department of Educational Studies at University of South Carolina in Columbia, SC. She served as codirector of the GEDI program during the 2009–2010 and 2010–2011 academic years.*

RITA O'SULLIVAN *is an associate professor of culture, curriculum, and change and director of Evaluation, Assessment, and Policy Connections at the University of North Carolina–Chapel Hill. She served as codirector of the GEDI program during the 2009–2010 and 2010–2011 academic years.*

New Directions for Evaluation • DOI: 10.1002/ev

Bertrand Jones, T. (2014). Socializing emerging evaluators: The use of mentoring to develop evaluation competence. In P. M. Collins & R. Hopson (Eds.), *Building a new generation of culturally responsive evaluators through AEA's Graduate Education Diversity Internship program. New Directions for Evaluation, 143*, 83–96.

6

Socializing Emerging Evaluators: The Use of Mentoring to Develop Evaluation Competence

Tamara Bertrand Jones

Abstract

The interdisciplinary nature of evaluation necessitates that emerging evaluators, those within the first five years in the evaluation profession, operate competently within the profession, and receive an extensive and deliberate socialization to the field. Mentoring is a key component to integrating these new evaluators into the field and one way that socialization takes place. In this chapter, survey data from GEDI participants are used to describe how the Graduate Education Diversity Internship (GEDI) program influences the socialization of diverse emerging scholars, specifically using mentoring relationships to facilitate the development of evaluation competence. Survey data exploring the interns' formal and informal mentoring relationships suggest that informal mentoring relationships were more effective and yield more support for psychosocial development and exposure to evaluation-related knowledge and competence in comparison with formal mentoring relationships. © Wiley Periodicals, Inc., and the American Evaluation Association.

As the demand for evaluation in progressively more diverse settings, programs, and stakeholders increases, the development of more evaluators, specifically, more evaluators of color, becomes one strategy to meet this increased demand (Frierson, 2000; Hood, 2000). The lived experiences of evaluators of color provide these professionals with a perspective that adds richness to design, technique, and reporting within evaluation settings (Hood, 2001; Tidwell, 1982). Often diverse evaluators approach the field from a variety of academic programs, ranging from public health to education, and as a result have extensive professional experiences. Consequently, the interdisciplinary nature of evaluation necessitates that emerging evaluators, those within the first five years in the evaluation profession, operate competently within the profession, and receive an extensive and deliberate socialization to the field.

Socialization is defined as a process that imparts the "knowledge, skills, and values necessary for successful entry into a professional career requiring an advanced level of specialized knowledge and skills" (Weidman, Twale, & Stein, 2001, p. iii). Emerging evaluators' socialization is influenced by practical evaluation experiences in the field, networking with evaluation professionals, and mentoring relationships with practicing evaluators (Bertrand, 2006). Collectively, these socialization experiences facilitate the development of evaluation knowledge and competence needed for success in the evaluation field. The purpose of this chapter is to describe how the Graduate Education Diversity Internship (GEDI) program influences the socialization of diverse emerging scholars, specifically using mentoring relationships to facilitate the development of evaluation competence.

Developing Evaluation Competence in Graduate School: The Graduate Education Diversity Internship

The American Evaluation Association's (2004) *Guiding Principles for Evaluators* highlight competence as one of the key values within which an evaluator must operate. At its core, the Competence principle refers to evaluators' proficient implementation of evaluation for stakeholders. The *Guiding Principles* urge:

> Evaluators should continually seek to maintain and improve their competencies, in order to provide the highest level of performance in their evaluations. This continuing professional development might include formal coursework and workshops, self-study, evaluations of one's own practice, and working with other evaluators to learn from their skills and expertise. (American Evaluation Association, 2004, Competence, para. 12.4)

Typically, emerging evaluators develop evaluation knowledge in graduate school and prior to the first evaluation position (Bertrand, 2006). For example, in a study of Black evaluators, 41% of the evaluators in the study conducted evaluations during graduate school. In describing the experience, evaluators expounded on the importance of the opportunity to practice their newfound skills during graduate training. Similarly, Stevens (2000) found that professional preparation, practical training, and working with a skilled mentor were essential for developing evaluation competence. These findings support the notion that education and practical training are key to increasing evaluation knowledge and contributing to competent evaluation practice.

The GEDI program is one example of the intentional blend of evaluation education and practical training. In 2000, AEA's Building Diversity Initiative (BDI) was initiated "to improve the quality and effectiveness of evaluation by expanding the ethnic and cultural diversity of the evaluation profession and by improving the capacity of evaluators to work across cultures" (American Evaluation Association, 2000, p. 1). As a result of the BDI, GEDI was developed to cultivate underrepresented evaluators.[1] Students in a variety of graduate programs were recruited to undergo extensive evaluation training. As part of the program interns were placed with agencies where they assisted with conducting evaluation.

Inherent in the Competence principle is the recognition of relationships among evaluators as central to developing evaluation-related competence. Evaluators are encouraged to "make every effort to gain the competence directly or through the assistance of others who possess the required expertise" (American Evaluation Association, 2004, Competence, para. 12.3). Likewise, the GEDI program also provided mentoring support for interns in the form of an advisor from the student's home institution and an active AEA member with similar research interests (Collins & Hopson, 2005).

Learning About Evaluation: Mentoring Relationships With Practicing Evaluators

Mentoring is a key component to integrating new members into a group and one way that socialization takes place (Cawyer, Simonds, & Davis, 2002; Chao, 2007; Davis, 2008). Mentoring relationships (mentorships) are defined as "dynamic, reciprocal, personal relationships in which a more experienced person (mentor) acts as a guide, role model, teacher, and sponsor of a less experienced person (protégé)" (Johnson & Ridley, 2004, p. xv). Mentoring is an act of "generativity—a process of bringing into existence and passing on a professional legacy" (p. xv). This interactive exchange of knowledge and competence is especially important for emerging evaluators.

Research on mentoring indicates that the process of mentoring helps emerging professionals learn technical expertise, become familiar with acceptable organizational or professional behavior, and develop a sense of competence. Benefits of mentoring for protégés include higher salaries, improved professional identity, greater professional competence, enhanced promotion rates, and accelerated career mobility (Johnson & Ridley, 2004). Outside of traditional dyads, individuals may develop relationships with multiple mentors, called mentoring networks (Wang, 2009). Mentoring networks, like mentoring dyads, provide even greater access to information, socialize one to the organizational culture, and enhance social capital (Jean-Marie & Brooks, 2011).

The two main functions of mentoring include career and psychosocial functions (Ragins & Kram, 2007). Career functions focus on career development and include behaviors that enhance career advancement (Ragins & Cotton, 1999). Psychosocial functions attend to interpersonal qualities of the mentorship and include behaviors that enhance professional and personal growth (Ragins & Cotton, 1999). When discussing mentoring relationships with faculty members and graduate students, Brown, Davis, and McClendon (1999) contended that both functions are important. They noted:

> The faculty member serves as a role model, teacher, sponsor, encourager, counselor, and friend to the students with the end goal of promoting the latter's professional and personal development. Each of these functions must be carried out within a context of a continuing, caring relationship between the mentor and mentee. (Brown et al., 1999, p. 113)

There are several factors that determine whether mentoring relationships provide career, psychosocial, or both functions. Among those factors include the protégé's needs, the mentor's ability to meet those needs, the mentor's needs, the chemistry in the relationship, and the organizational context (Ragins, 1997, as cited in Ragins & Kram, 2007). The same mentor may provide different functions to different protégés (Ragins & Kram, 2007).

Two types of mentoring relationships, formal and informal, occur and each can influence the outcomes of the relationship (Ragins & Cotton, 1999). Formal relationships are those that have been arranged by an organization or other entity. In formal mentorships mentors and protégés are typically matched based on some criteria determined by program staff and are less likely to be founded on "mutual perceptions of competency and respect" (Ragins & Cotton, 1999, p. 531). The authors report research on mentoring that suggests formal relationships typically last between six months and one year. In formal relationships the degree of trust and emotional closeness is lessened when compared to informal relationships.

Informal relationships are those that develop between individuals without external assistance. These mentorships usually begin based on mutual identification and fulfill career needs (Ragins & Cotton, 1999). Informal relationships typically last between three and six years, depending on the needs of those involved. Consequently, in informal relationships the psychosocial functions identified above are more likely to occur than in formal relationships. Many of the GEDI program participants formed formal mentoring relationships with senior evaluators. These interns were assigned, by GEDI program staff, an experienced evaluator as a mentor. In addition, interns developed informal mentoring relationships with evaluators they met during program activities.

Capturing the Influence of Evaluation Mentoring Relationships

To learn more about the interns' socialization experiences, GEDI participants completed a modified version of the *Evaluation Professional Survey* (Bertrand, 2006). The descriptive survey focused on participants' socialization into the evaluation field through the GEDI program; respondents were asked about their academic preparation in graduate school (i.e., specific evaluation courses completed) and the mentoring that occurred throughout both the participant's graduate program and GEDI participation. Mentoring takes up almost half of the survey, with 37 items. The skip logic built into the survey allowed participants to avoid items that were not relevant to their mentoring experiences. As a result, response time for the entire survey ranged from nine minutes to one hour. Email addresses were obtained from program staff for previous GEDI participants from Cohorts 1–9, 62 individuals in total. Electronic mail invitations were sent soliciting their participation in the survey. The findings from the mentoring portion of the survey will be presented. To maintain anonymity of GEDI interns, any references to a specific mentor or agency have been replaced with a pseudonym. Additionally, cohort identification is included except in cases where intern anonymity would be compromised.

GEDI Intern Demographics

As of October 2013, 62 GEDI interns in nine cohorts had completed the program. Twenty-two respondents from each of the previous nine cohorts were represented in the survey respondents, resulting in a 36% response rate. Twelve of the 22 respondents were African American, three Latino/a, five Asian/Asian Americans, and two respondents did not provide their race/ethnicity. Seventeen respondents were female and five male. Seven of the participants were completing master's degrees and the remaining 15 participants were pursuing doctorate degrees while participating in GEDI. On average, respondents' demographics mirror the overall GEDI program participants. Table 6.1 details the GEDI cohort, cohort size, and the number of respondents.

GEDI participants were asked about their formal mentoring experiences, those mentorships assigned by the program, as well as about the mentors who were not assigned through the program, the informal relationships. The majority of the GEDI respondents ($n = 14$) were assigned a mentor through the GEDI program. In some cases, GEDI interns also developed informal mentorships with evaluators. Additionally, nine of the 14 who were assigned a mentor developed both formal relationships and informal relationships. As the relationships varied in the demographics of the

Table 6.1. Cohort Respondents

Cohort	Cohort Size	Respondents
Cohort 1 (2004–2005)	4	2
Cohort 2 (2005–2006)	4	1
Cohort 3 (2006–2007)	8	3
Cohort 4 (2007–2008)	9	3
Cohort 5 (2008–2009)	7	3
Cohort 6 (2009–2010)	9	5
Cohort 7 (2010–2011)	8	1
Cohort 8 (2011–2012)	7	3
Cohort 9 (2012–2013)	6	1
Total	62	22

Table 6.2. Mentor Functions: A Comparison of Formal and Informal Mentors

Mentor Functions	GEDI Mentors	
	Formal	Informal
Career advice	6	14
Ways to develop evaluation competence	8	8
Appropriate professional conduct/behavior	6	8
Support for personal development	7	12
Evaluation/research opportunities	7	11
Assistance/advice for work-related issues	10	14
Assistance/advice for personal/social issues	4	8

mentors and the identified benefits based on the type of relationship, the formal mentoring relationships will be discussed, followed by the informal mentoring relationships. Table 6.2 details the mentor functions in both formal and informal relationships. GEDI interns who indicated both informal and formal relationships were included in each category.

Formal Evaluation Mentoring: GEDI-Facilitated Relationships

The demographics of formal mentors varied. Some interns were assigned a White female ($n = 4$) or a Black female mentor ($n = 5$), while other interns were assigned male mentors—two White and three Black.

Short-term versus long-term mentoring. GEDI interns were asked to report the length of their mentoring relationships using a scale that included less than one year, 1–3 years, 4–6 years, 7–9 years, and 10 or more years. The mentoring relationships developed between students and their GEDI mentors lasted on average one to three years. Throughout the time of the relationships, participants contacted mentors via email and telephone, as well as meeting face to face at the AEA conferences or GEDI trainings. Some mentoring dyads communicated as frequently as monthly, others less frequently or annually. Over half of the interns who were assigned mentors through the GEDI program continued their relationships after GEDI ended. For those relationships that continued after the GEDI program, interns identified collaboration on evaluation work, dissertation research, or publications helped to fuel their relationship. One Cohort 1 intern noted, "We continued to do work together. The mentor served on my dissertation committee and I worked with him on a project." When asked why their mentoring relationships did not continue after the GEDI program, interns cited reasons, including personal and mentor schedule conflicts, and no longer working in evaluation.

Mentor functions. GEDI formal mentors provided both career-related and psychosocial functions in the mentorships with their protégés. While both functions were identified, the majority of protégés acknowledged the career development related functions more than the psychosocial functions. Likewise, respondents indicated that developing evaluation competence and assistance/advice for work-related issues were the most popular topics discussed with their mentors.

Interns were asked to identify, as a check all that apply item on the survey, the skills they learned and the ways the formal mentor contributed to their development as an evaluator. The numbers in Table 6.2 represent respondents who received the identified support from their mentor. The majority of interns noted their improved evaluation competence and the opportunity for and increased skill related to networking as benefits of the formal mentoring relationships. A Black male intern identified ways the mentor influenced his evaluation competence, noting specific skills he gained, including "avoiding the inclination to stop at superficial levels of understanding; managing a basic evaluation project; use of organizing tools and coding for data management and analysis." Another Black male intern said, "My mentor provided an understanding, supportive, and knowledgeable resource for development of my early understanding of applied evaluation activities."

Similarly, several interns identified the importance of psychosocial functions in their mentoring relationships, specifically noting the mentor's influence in increasing their confidence. For example, one Latina intern noted, "She [the mentor] believed in my potential." One Black female intern described the role her mentor played in assisting her to develop evaluation competence and increasing her confidence, a psychosocial function. She noted, "My evaluation skills improved exponentially as a result of my mentor. I am much more confident as an evaluator." Another Black female intern also commented on her mentor's contribution to building her confidence.

> My mentor helped me to navigate working for a consulting firm once I was out of grad school. She gave me encouragement and general tips about the environment (which came in handy since I came from a nonprofit background).

She also gave me information on the challenges of working and getting a PhD, but also the confidence to make my way in evaluation without a PhD.

Networking was identified as another benefit of formal evaluation mentoring. Interns not only noted the opportunity to network but also the improved networking skills, including the confidence needed to approach senior evaluators, that developed as a result of their formal mentoring. One Latina intern acknowledged, "Being a GEDI gives you the skills to collaborate with others. It positions you as a professional in the field. I was fortunate to work with a team at [ABC] that valued my contributions as a researcher/evaluator." A Black female intern discussed an increased comfort in approaching her mentor in other settings, stating, "I was able to meet with and network my mentor and would feel comfortable approaching him in other evaluation settings."

Conflicting views on formal mentoring. There were mixed results of the formal mentoring received in the GEDI program. Some interns spoke highly of the formal mentoring, while others identified the formal mentoring as an area of improvement for the program. One Cohort 4 intern positively noted:

The GEDI program is one of the most influential programs of my graduate career—if not the most influential. I grew as a graduate student and as a scholar. I also learned valuable skills which I apply almost daily in my professional life. My GEDI experience exposed me to scholars in the field, including those that assisted in my dissertation process. It also helped me to establish life-long relationships with individuals that now serve as part of my professional support network.

Similarly, another Cohort 4 intern said:

The GEDI program is a vital opportunity in the development of emerging evaluation scholars. By providing aspiring evaluators an opportunity to receive training, engage evaluation field leaders, acquire and apply new knowledge, the GEDI program is an unmatched experience. Additionally, by providing this opportunity with the support of individuals who acknowledge the diverse perspectives the participants bring to the program a space that celebrates the important contribution diversity plays in evaluation is celebrated.

Other interns, who were also assigned a formal mentor, disagreed about the utility of the mentoring they received. The interns who expressed dissatisfaction with the mentoring relationships were also those who did not continue their relationships after the program's conclusion. For example, one Cohort 1 intern reported:

NEW DIRECTIONS FOR EVALUATION • DOI: 10.1002/ev

The GEDI program, in terms of the guidance provided and regular meetings, is wonderful. The only part I didn't like was the required mentor. Mentoring relationships grow out of an initial spark, shared interests, etc. and not out of requirements.

Another intern from Cohort 6 expressed similar sentiments.

The mentoring component of the GEDI program is also not the strongest component, which I think is ok. In other words, the networking, training, and professional development in GEDI are sufficient without a formal mentoring relationship in my opinion.

GEDI interns engaged in formal mentoring relationships identified the importance of these relationships in increasing their evaluation knowledge and personal confidence in conducting evaluation. Despite the different perceptions of the strength of the formal mentors assigned by the GEDI program, most interns agreed on the influence of these relationships in strengthening their thinking about evaluation-related ideas and increasing their professional networks.

Informal Evaluation Mentoring: Non-GEDI-Facilitated Relationships

Many of the important mentoring relationships developed in the GEDI program were informal. These relationships were not assigned, per se, by the GEDI program staff, but were facilitated because of exposure to these evaluators during GEDI-sponsored programs and activities. Fourteen GEDI interns confirmed developing informal mentoring relationships outside the confines of the GEDI program, most of them developed during graduate school. Unlike the formal mentoring relationships, the majority of the informal mentoring relationships were developed with Black males ($n = 7$), followed by White females ($n = 3$), White males ($n = 2$), a Black female, and a Latino male. Using the same scale identified earlier, GEDI interns reported these mentoring relationships lasting on average one to three years.

Benefits of informal mentoring relationships. Like the formal mentoring relationships, interns identified increased evaluation knowledge as a result of the informal relationships. GEDI interns named specific career-related skills such as "how to use and develop various evaluation tools," "the fundamentals of culturally relevant/competent evaluation," and "how to write evaluation proposals." One Latina intern explained, "I have become very competent regarding the theory and practice of culturally responsive evaluation." Additionally, other interns discussed evaluation-related competence including knowledge related to "current structure of government evaluation and performance measurement," and "assessing gaps in skills and prioritizing the competencies for professional development."

NEW DIRECTIONS FOR EVALUATION • DOI: 10.1002/ev

GEDI interns also mentioned the psychosocial benefits to their informal mentorships. Reflecting on the relationship with their mentor, one intern labeled these "soft skills." The soft skills included "confidence," "perseverance," "persistence," "professionalism," "teamwork," "collaboration," "communication," and "organization." Similarly, another intern noted that their mentor helped them develop "the ability to look for opportunities and open doors with every obstacle." In addition to specific skills identified, interns also spoke of other personal and professional skills that were influenced by the relationships with their informal mentor, like "learning 'the game'" and "taking advantage of opportunities for networking." As mentioned previously, some interns were working toward a master's degree while participating in GEDI. A Black female intern spoke of her mentor's assistance during the doctoral admission process among other helpful tasks. During the GEDI program she was pursuing a master's degree and acknowledged her mentor's assistance with "navigating the professional environment, narrowing down my interests, building confidence in my path, PhD application assistance."

Mentor functions. In discussing the non-GEDI mentoring, interns were overwhelmingly positive. Similar to the formal mentorships, the interns identified both career-related and psychosocial functions fulfilled by their mentors. One Black female intern noted, "He has made me a well-rounded person—not just someone with technical skills—but also a 'human being' who happens to work in evaluation."

An intern from Cohort 6 acknowledged:

> No other mentor or school/work experiences prepared me for the organizational setting and the dynamics of the workplace. In addition to teaching me evaluation on my jobs, he has taught me this as well as how to advance myself professionally.

Another intern from Cohort 6 confirmed:

> He's my career lifeline it seems! Sometimes I think I bug him too much, but he is very responsive and encouraging. He wants me to be happy and successful. I don't know where my career would be if it wasn't for him!

One intern from Cohort 5 discussed the support and challenge provided by her informal mentor. She noted, "My mentor provided an excellent balance of building up and being hands-off so I could address my own challenges. He also fills in whatever resources I might need, through his own expertise or a contact of his."

Formal and Informal Mentoring: Socializing New Evaluators

From the responses of former GEDI interns, formal and informal mentoring relationships incorporated both career and psychosocial functions. While the informal mentoring relationships provided more career-related and personal development, the formal relationships focused more on evaluation knowledge and competence and career-related advice. There could be several reasons for the differential outcomes based on the type of relationship. Ragins and Cotton (1999) noted that informal and formal mentoring relationships differ in many ways, including length of the relationship, reason for initiating the relationship, and outcomes based on the relationship. The GEDI mentoring relationships mirror these differences as well.

For example, more interns who developed informal relationships indicated their mentors provided more personal support than GEDIs in formal mentoring relationships. Further examination of the intern responses indicates a nuanced personal relationship with their informal relationship that in turn influenced the intern's evaluation-related competence. It was through the relationship that developed with their mentor that increased their confidence and ultimately influenced increased evaluation skill. This finding supports the notion in the mentoring literature that the psychosocial functions of mentoring may appear less in formal relationships (Ragins & Cotton, 1999).

Contrary to existing research, GEDIs' formal mentoring relationships lasted longer than typical formal mentoring relationships. Ragins and Cotton (1999) reported that most formal mentoring relationships lasted between six months and one year, while the GEDI respondents noted their formal relationships lasting on average one to three years. The GEDI informal mentorships reportedly lasted between three and six years which align with the expected time frame for formal relationships.

One Cohort 1 intern's comment provides food for thought on why her formal mentoring relationship was not successful. She noted, "It is hard to develop a mentoring relationship online/long-distance. It felt strained and like we were fulfilling part of the GEDI requirement as opposed to something that developed organically." The intern's thoughts, along with the data about the GEDI intern mentoring relationships, provide additional considerations for the GEDI program's mentoring function, as well as how future mentoring programs might be structured.

The data also support previous research that informal mentoring is different than formal mentoring. The GEDI reflections point out that both formal and informal mentoring are needed to provide the exposure that emerging evaluators need. In developing formal mentoring programs, a suggestion by Ragins and Cotton (1999) has merit for the GEDI program and other programs like it. Using a formal mentor pairing to springboard into an informal mentorship allows participants the best of both worlds. Interns would receive the career development and psychosocial support acquired from both types of relationships, and experience many of the benefits of career sponsorship and organizational support more likely to be provided in formal relationships.

Limitations of the Data

There are several limitations to the data presented in this chapter. Despite the representation from each of the nine cohorts, the data presented only reflect the experiences and perceptions of the GEDI interns who responded to the survey. Caution should be used when applying the findings of all GEDI interns. Another limitation includes the data collection tool used. Interns were asked to reflect on their mentorship with one mentor, while there may have been many mentors that impacted development of their evaluation-related knowledge. Additionally, a survey provided limited space for respondents to expound upon their experiences. The nuances of the mentorship, particularly the individual perspectives influencing the perceptions of this relationship, are not captured. Individual interviews or focus groups with GEDI interns could potentially provide richer data, at the very least the researcher could ask probing or follow-up questions to allow participants to explain their responses.

Implications for the Field

Changes in our society's demographic makeup and multiple social identities underscore the demand for culturally diverse and aware professionals, particularly in evaluation. Through academic preparation, professional development through practical field experiences, and intentional networking with and mentoring from knowledgeable professionals, emerging evaluators develop evaluation knowledge and expertise. The GEDI program provided mentoring and professional development for underrepresented evaluators to complement academic preparation received during graduate training, all with an emphasis on culturally responsive evaluation. Data from the interns confirm that the GEDI program provides an opportunity to socialize emerging evaluators into the evaluation field. Participants in the GEDI receive access to formal and informal mentors and mentorships that influences evaluation-related competence and socialization to the evaluation profession required to become knowledgeable evaluators that can ultimately influence the field.

The advantages of informal mentoring relationships involve their longer duration, and slightly greater balance of both psychosocial and career-related functions. This balance of the impersonal (career) with the personal (psychosocial) creates a more holistic approach to not only mentoring but also to broader socialization of emerging evaluators. In essence, attention to this perspective encourages development of "human beings who happen to work in evaluation." Boyd Cowles (2005) encouraged evaluators to step beyond traditional comfort zones to create "authentic, trusting, and honest relationships" (p. 15). Socialization experiences, including mentoring and professional development, with an equal emphasis on protégés'

NEW DIRECTIONS FOR EVALUATION • DOI: 10.1002/ev

evaluation-related competence and personal development create an opportunity for greater impact on the evaluator and the profession.

Pipeline programs, like the Graduate Education Diversity Internship program, provide a demonstrable commitment to increasing the numbers of multicultural evaluators. The program signifies a commitment to creating an evaluation community that is reflective of our society at large. These programs provide evaluation capacity building, assist in shifting organizational culture, and ensure the sustainability of our profession. The preparation from the Graduate Education Diversity Internship program provided at the graduate level impacts emerging evaluators' ability to conduct sound evaluation and integrate culturally responsive evaluative thought into their evaluation practice. Developing competently trained and socialized evaluators with diverse identities adds to the credibility of the evaluation field. The emphasis on developing individuals with not only evaluation competency but also the skills to navigate various cultural settings ensures the continued and improved quality of evaluation.

Note

1. For more details about the development and purpose of the GEDI program, see Collins, Kirkhart, and Brown (Chapter 2 of this issue).

References

American Evaluation Association. (2000). *AEA building diversity initiative*. Retrieved from http://www.eval.org/p/cm/ld/fid=131

American Evaluation Association. (2004). *Guiding principles for evaluators*. Retrieved from http://www.eval.org/p/cm/ld/fid=51

Bertrand, T. C. (2006). *Cultural competency in evaluation: A Black perspective* (Doctoral dissertation). Retrieved from ProQuest Dissertations and Theses website: http://search.proquest.com/docview/305334395

Boyd Cowles, T. (2005). Ten strategies for enhancing multicultural competency in evaluation. *The Evaluation Exchange, 11*(2), 15, 19.

Brown, M. C., Davis, G. L., & McClendon, S. A. (1999). Mentoring graduate students of color: Myths, models, and modes. *Peabody Journal of Education, 74*(2), 105–118.

Cawyer, C. S., Simonds, C., & Davis, S. (2002). Mentoring to facilitate socialization: The case of the new faculty member. *International Journal of Qualitative Studies in Education, 15*(2), 225–242.

Chao, G. T. (2007). Mentoring and organizational socialization: Networks for work adjustment. In B. R. Ragins & K. E. Kram (Eds.), *The handbook of mentoring at work: Theory, research, and practice* (pp. 179–196). Thousand Oaks, CA: Sage.

Collins, P., & Hopson, R. K. (2005). Beyond basic training: Building a pipeline program for evaluators of color. *The Evaluation Exchange, 11*(2), 17, 19.

Davis, D. J. (2008). Mentorship and the socialization of underrepresented minorities into the professoriate: Examining varied influences. *Mentoring & Tutoring: Partnership in Learning, 16*(3), 278–293.

Frierson, H. T. (2000). The need for the participation of minority professionals in educational evaluation. In E. Johnson (Ed.), *The cultural context of educational evaluation:*

The role of minority evaluation professionals (pp. 48–52). Arlington, VA: National Science Foundation.

Hood, S. (2000). New look at an old question. In E. Johnson (Ed.), *The cultural context of educational evaluation: The role of minority evaluation professionals* (pp. 28–31). Arlington, VA: National Science Foundation.

Hood, S. (2001). Nobody knows my name: In praise of African American evaluators who were responsive. In J. C. Greene & T. A. Abma (Eds.), *New Directions for Evaluation: No. 92. Responsive evaluation* (pp. 31–43). San Francisco, CA: Jossey-Bass. doi:10.1002/ev.33

Jean-Marie, G., & Brooks, J. S. (2011). Mentoring and supportive networks for women of color in academe. In G. Jean-Marie & B. Lloyd-Jones (Eds.), *Women of color in higher education: Changing directions and new perspectives* (Diversity in Higher Education, 10, 91–108). Bingley, UK: Emerald Group Publishing Limited.

Johnson, W. B., & Ridley, C. R. (2004). *The elements of mentoring*. New York, NY: Palgrave Macmillan.

Ragins, B. R., & Cotton, J. L. (1999). Mentor functions and outcomes: A comparison of men and women in formal and informal mentoring relationships. *Journal of Applied Psychology, 84*(4), 529–550.

Ragins, B. R., & Kram, K. E. (Eds.). (2007). *The handbook of mentoring at work: Theory, research, and practice*. Thousand Oaks, CA: Sage.

Stevens, F. I. (2000). Reflections and interviews: Information collected about training minority evaluators of math and science projects. In E. Johnson (Ed.), *The cultural context of educational evaluation: The role of minority evaluation professionals* (pp. 41–47). Arlington, VA: National Science Foundation.

Tidwell, R. (1982). Four dilemmas faced by Black investigators. *Journal of Black Studies, 13*(2), 241–252.

Wang, J. (2009). Networking in the workplace: Implications for women's career development. In C. R. Nanton & M. V. Alfred (Eds.), *New Directions for Adult and Continuing Education: No. 122. Social capital and women's support systems: Networking, learning, and surviving* (pp. 33–42). San Francisco, CA: Jossey-Bass.

Weidman, J. C., Twale, D. J., & Stein, E. L. (2001). *Socialization of graduate and professional students in higher education: A perilous passage [ASHE-ERIC Higher Education Report, 28(3)]*. Washington, DC: Graduate School of Education and Human Development, The George Washington University.

TAMARA BERTRAND JONES *is an assistant professor of higher education at Florida State University.*

Lee, K., & Gilbert, B. (2014). Embedding the Graduate Education Diversity Internship (GEDI) program within a larger system. In P. M. Collins & R. Hopson (Eds.), *Building a new generation of culturally responsive evaluators through AEA's Graduate Education Diversity Internship program. New Directions for Evaluation, 143,* 97–108.

7

Embedding the Graduate Education Diversity Internship (GEDI) Program Within a Larger System

Kien Lee, Brandi Gilbert

Abstract

This chapter discusses the systemic changes that need to occur in order for the Graduate Education Diversity Internship (GEDI) to live up to its mission and the underlying values for which it stands. It examines the context within which the GEDI program was created and the values and norms that shaped the program curriculum, followed by an examination of the organizations that comprise the ecosystem that shapes the evaluation profession. It concludes with suggestions for impacting this ecosystem and more important, the acknowledgement of the ecosystem that requires pipeline programs like the GEDI program to focus on change beyond the individual level. © Wiley Periodicals, Inc., and the American Evaluation Association.

Introduction

This chapter represents the perspective of an organization that supports the Graduate Education Diversity Internship (GEDI) program and employs evaluators, including several graduates of the program. It is a perspective about what would make an ideal employer–employee match for GEDI program graduates, including the attributes of the employer and the competencies of the program graduate. The authors use this perspective to demonstrate the changes that need to occur across all the organizations that have a role in supporting the GEDI program in order to live up to the mission of the program.

As part of the discussion, the authors have to first examine the context within which the GEDI program was created and continues to operate. This context includes the changing demographics of communities in the United States that made it necessary to have such a program, and the values and norms that support traditional research designs (e.g., experimental and quasi-experimental designs), which do not appreciate the role of culture in evaluation. The context also includes the organizations that make up the ecosystem that can help drive the success of the GEDI program as well as fulfill the program's larger mission—to level the evaluation playing field for professionals of color and to deepen the thinking and discussion about the role of culture in evaluation. The organizations include the institution that manages the program (first Duquesne University, followed by the University of North Carolina-Chapel Hill, and now Claremont Graduate University); the American Evaluation Association (AEA); the interns' academic institution; the host organizations where the interns apply their evaluation knowledge and skills; the places that employ the interns after they graduate; and the public, private, and nonprofit organizations that fund and use evaluation.

Both authors of this chapter bring unique insights into this discussion. The first author was involved in the implementation of the American Evaluation Association Building Diversity Initiative (BDI), which led to the creation of the GEDI program, and as an employer of evaluation professionals, including several GEDI program graduates. The second author is a GEDI graduate.

Why the GEDI Program Was—and Still Is—Necessary

The BDI, which took place between 2000 and 2001, was funded by the W. K. Kellogg Foundation; led by AEA by way of a project oversight committee comprised of selected board members and leaders in the profession; and managed and implemented by Community Science (then Association for the Study and Development of Community). The reason for the BDI, out of which the GEDI program grew, was very compelling. Ricardo Millett, who at that time was the evaluator manager for the Kellogg Foundation, had been receiving feedback from private funders that they were struggling with finding evaluators of color. These funders, who were paying increasing attention to the racial, ethnic, and cultural diversity of communities and the impact of this diversity on neighborhoods, institutions, and systems, assumed that evaluators who shared the racial, ethnic, and cultural characteristics of program participants would yield more culturally relevant and valid evaluations (Association for the Study and Development of Community [ASDC], 2002). This assumption supports the line of reasoning that increasing the number of people in a traditionally underrepresented group could have positive outcomes on issues associated with the disproportional representation in the first place (Deaux & Ullman, 1983; Toren & Kraus, 1987). This assumption also demanded a particular response from the evaluation profession—a larger pool of racially, ethnically, and culturally diverse evaluators. This demand compelled Dr. Millett to fund the BDI (see Symonette, Hopson, & Mertens, Chapter 1 of this issue, for details about the historical framing of BDI).

The recommendations that emerged from the BDI can be broadly categorized as: creation of a pipeline for evaluators of color, training programs to develop culturally competent evaluators, increased access to resources and opportunities for evaluators of color (e.g., job announcements, requests for evaluation consultants), and organizational changes in AEA that support the profession's diversification and institutionalization of culturally competent evaluation practices (ASDC, 2000). These recommendations reflect the perspective that increasing the number of people from traditionally underrepresented groups in any profession is critical, but not sufficient, in order to improve racial equity in the United States in general.

The GEDI program emerged from the recommendation to create a pipeline. The original suggestion was a graduate education fellowship program targeted to students of color. This recommendation stirred a lot of controversy among AEA's board leadership at the time, as observed and experienced by former board members who had worked on the BDI as well as the staff members at Community Science who were responsible for the BDI. The board leadership believed that the fellowship program should consider forms of diversity other than race and ethnicity (e.g., geographic distribution across the country, academic discipline, research methodology), and did not embrace the important role that racial and ethnic diversity play in helping to ensure evaluations that are responsive to the needs of communities of color. (Note: The leadership that supported the BDI had completed their terms and been replaced by new board members who were not as supportive of the effort.) In the end, the board consented to an internship program that they perceived to be less controversial and less costly to implement than a fellowship program. The result was the GEDI program, a first-time event for AEA that has thus far trained more than 60 graduate students of color in evaluation. This experience further highlighted the importance of ensuring a pipeline of board candidates who are committed to the role of evaluation in promoting social justice in order to ensure the sustainability of such efforts.

Role of Culture in Evaluation

Traditional evaluation practices, which have their roots in the postpositivist paradigm, are capable only of quantitatively measuring program outcomes, based on more or less established measures, and describing the context within which the program operated (Hood, 2004). Thus, traditional evaluation practices cannot adequately account for the dynamic interaction between the program and the contextual variables that affect its implementation and outcomes, the various ways to define a success measure, the apprehensiveness toward research and evaluation by communities of color who have had negative experiences with the findings, and the power structures that exclude people of color from giving their input (in a nontokenistic way; see Thompson-Robinson, Hopson, & SenGupta, 2004). While the shift toward more culturally responsive methodologies continues, some public agencies and private foundations insist on evaluations that use experimental or quasi-experimental methodologies, despite their incompatibility for the environments within which the evaluands are expected to operate (SenGupta, Hopson, & Thompson-Robinson, 2004).

Culturally responsive evaluation requires close attention to stakeholder engagement, especially stakeholders who have traditionally been excluded. It is important that these stakeholders' values, traditions, norms, languages, social institutions, and needs be considered in the evaluation design and process. Also, the evaluation should not overemphasize their deficiencies, but instead build on their strengths or assets. To be able to pay attention to all these considerations, evaluators must be mindful of their implicit biases (see Thomas & Stevens, 2004). Additionally, the proper use of the findings (i.e., compliance with AEA's Guiding Principles D [Respect for People] and E [Responsibilities for General and Public Welfare]) is a very critical consideration in culturally responsive evaluation because certain socially excluded groups have been harmed by studies conducted about them.

Close attention to the above elements demands, at the individual and organizational levels, a certain set of attributes, including a commitment to social justice; the self-resolve to reflect on one's worldview and perceptions of people from a different racial, ethnic, and cultural group; and the fortitude to face and challenge asymmetric power relations. Sufficient time and resources (monetary and human) must be allocated in the evaluation to properly engage people, and evaluators must have the ability to facilitate group processes (Symonette, 2004). The tolerance, acceptance, or valuing of these attributes will depend on the organization where evaluation is desired, practiced, and/or consumed, including government agencies, community-based organizations, nonprofit or for-profit consulting companies, academic institutions, and foundations. As such, these organizations as well as AEA and the interns' host institutions play a critical role in ensuring that culture is explicitly and seriously considered in evaluations. The roles of these organizations are discussed in the next section.

The Ecosystem of Organizations That Can Change the Status Quo

Figure 7.1 illustrates the ecosystem of organizations in helping to change the status quo in evaluation by supporting pipeline programs like the GEDI

Figure 7.1. Constellation of Organizations That Help Drive the Success of the GEDI Program

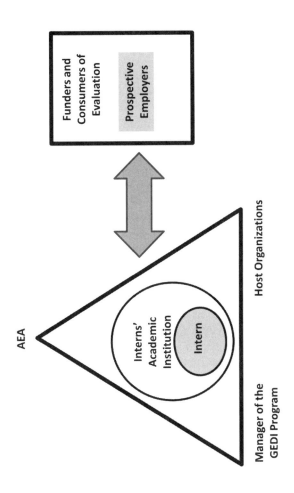

program, level the evaluation playing field for professionals of color, and ensure that communities of color are not harmed by evaluation by funding or demanding culturally responsive evaluations. The underlying logic presumes that as national professional associations such as AEA, academic institutions, and organizations promote the importance of culturally responsive evaluation by preparing professionals skilled in its practice, the diffusion of culturally responsive evaluation occurs. This diffusion in turn increases the demand for such evaluation by funders and consumer of evaluation. In the long term, this iterative cycle of change and ecosystem of organizations have the potential to contribute to racial equity at the societal level.

AEA. AEA has supported the GEDI program as a fiscal partner and has provided training opportunities for interns through its annual conferences and professional development workshops. Also, as the national professional association for evaluators in the United States, AEA has the power to influence and shape the practice of evaluation. By reflecting on its policies and processes to ensure that they promote diversity, inclusion, and equity, it can encourage people of color to join the profession and influence funders and consumers' demand for culturally responsive evaluations.

Administrators of the GEDI program. The GEDI program has been managed by evaluators and researchers based in academic institutions (first Duquesne University, followed by the University of North Carolina-Chapel Hill, and now, Claremont Graduate University). The GEDI program administrator manages the recruitment of interns; facilitates training opportunities for them; serves as liaison between them and potential host institutions and employers; and fosters a sense of community among GEDI program alumni, interns, and formal and informal mentors from the field of evaluation. Equally as important, the GEDI program administrator advocates for diversifying the evaluation profession.

Interns' academic institution. Each intern identifies a faculty advisor to support the interns' participation in the program. This may include assisting the students with integrating principles of culturally responsive evaluation into their own research or evaluation work in their academic program, supporting their attendance and other forms of involvement at AEA, and helping them reflect on and process their experiences.

Host organizations. In order for GEDI interns to gain hands-on evaluation experience, they are placed in host institutions that serve as fiscal partners and provide opportunities for interns to work on an evaluation project. These placements enable interns to apply their evaluation skills, from developing evaluation plans to data analysis, report writing, and client management. Host organizations have included universities, nonprofit organizations, for-profit consulting firms, and foundations. Some of the host organizations have an explicit commitment to diversity, inclusion, and equity, and thus are aligned with the GEDI program goals. Other host organizations have demonstrated little interest or capacity in confronting issues related to diversity, inclusion, and equity; hosting an intern merely provides them with an emerging professional with basic evaluation knowledge and skills.

Prospective employers. Prospective employers of GEDI program graduates include government agencies, community-based organizations, nonprofit or for-profit consulting companies, academic institutions, and foundations. Similar to the host organizations, the degree of compatibility between GEDI program graduates and employers depends, in part, on the GEDI program administrator's brokering of the relationship and arrangement through existing members of AEA as well as the marketability of the graduates' competencies.

Organizations that fund and use evaluation. These organizations include government agencies, community-based organizations, nonprofit or for-profit consulting companies, academic institutions, and foundations. Funders and consumers of evaluation play an integral role in promoting diversity, inclusion, and equity in the practice of evaluation. Funders can increase the demand for culturally responsive evaluations by intentionally requiring it in their requests for proposals, while consumers can demand it by challenging evaluators about their assumptions and practices. Ultimately, the demands by funders and consumers could increase the likelihood of evaluators taking a culturally competent and responsive evaluation approach, and thus help to reduce harm on communities of color.

As described above, the organizations each have a unique role in supporting pipeline programs like the GEDI program, leveling the evaluation playing field for professionals of color, and ensuring that communities of color are not harmed by evaluation. They form an ecosystem where if one of these types of organizations, for whatever reason, fails to recognize or undervalues the importance of diversity, inclusion, and equity, the diversification of the evaluation profession and widespread practice of culturally responsive evaluation would be difficult to achieve.

The next section discusses the ecosystem from the perspective of a prospective employer, starting with what the authors believe, based on their experiences, are the essential characteristics of GEDI program graduates that prospective employers must value in order for a successful match and working relationship.

The Ecosystem That Supports (or Does Not Support) the GEDI Program

GEDI graduates and their prospective employers have to share two critical characteristics to maintain a successful relationship, including:

- Explicit commitment to promoting equity for communities of color and interest in using evaluation to support this commitment; and

New Directions for Evaluation • DOI: 10.1002/ev

- Explicit commitment to culturally responsive evaluation and knowledge and skills in designing and implementing such evaluations.

This commitment to the link between evaluation and equity is an inherent part of the GEDI program; it is implied through the GEDI program's goal to diversify the evaluation profession and the training curriculum. Organizations that employ GEDI graduates would ideally share the same commitment and values about the role that evaluation plays in generating knowledge that can be used to promote equity (as opposed to evaluation that is used solely to determine the merits of a program or initiative). As well, they would share the same commitment to practicing evaluation that is responsive to the stakeholders whose views are often excluded, ignored, or dismissed; this tends to be stakeholders from racial, ethnic, and cultural minority groups. Without this shared value, GEDI graduates could become frustrated because they would be unable to live up to the commitment to promote equity and may not have the coaching or other support to develop and practice the required skills.

A critical question for the GEDI program administrator and the GEDI program graduate is whether or not the prospective employer is "ready" for the perspectives that the graduate brings. It would be safe to assume that most individuals who become part of a pipeline program specifically for professionals of color have experienced exclusion and seek to improve their access to the resources and opportunities that can advance their careers. Whether through their experiences prior to or during their participation in the pipeline program, they learn about the institutional barriers that help to maintain or even perpetuate racial and ethnic inequities. This experience and knowledge is likely to affect the way they think about, evaluate, and explain an intervention in order to ensure that racial bias and structural barriers are accounted for in the evaluation design and interpretation of findings. Are prospective employers that typically fund and conduct large evaluations that reflect more traditional paradigms "ready" to engage with the perspective that evaluation plays a role in addressing inequity?

In addition to the link between evaluation and equity, there is also a need for GEDI graduates and their prospective employers to share an explicit commitment to culturally responsive evaluation and knowledge and skills in designing and implementing evaluations. GEDI interns undergo an intensive training program where they learn about evaluation and the role of culture in evaluation. A culturally responsive evaluation, as mentioned before, requires sufficient funds, time to plan properly, skills in community outreach and engagement, and knowledge about the social structures of certain groups of people—capacities that need to be negotiated according to the terms of agreement between the evaluator and the client. These terms of agreement can be difficult to negotiate if the client is not committed to the principles of culturally responsive evaluation. A prospective employer that cares about the role of culture in evaluation provides a fertile ground for GEDI graduates to learn more about how to negotiate these terms.

Anecdotal reports from some GEDI graduates suggest that they have encountered resistance to the practice of such evaluations in the organizations that employ them, and were at a loss as to how to address this resistance because until then they had been engaged with professionals who understand and value the role of culture in evaluation. The GEDI program administrator may want to consider strengthening the GEDI program curriculum by adding additional training about what it takes to be a change agent in order to better prepare GEDI program graduates to deal with and overcome the resistance they might encounter. This could involve role plays, debates about the value-added of culturally responsive evaluation, and engaging with professionals (e.g., facilitated discussions with nonprofit leaders, evaluators, funders) who are perhaps less inclined toward such evaluation. In particular, GEDI program interns might want to learn more about how to reflect on and respond to decisions and actions that are counter to their culturally relevant values and practices, and adjust their language to respond to intended audience (see Grant & Oswick, 2010 for a discussion about how individuals can become change agents in organizations).

Readiness of the evaluation field for what the GEDI program truly stands for. The first part of this chapter described why the GEDI program was necessary, from assumptions about the importance of racial and ethnic congruence between evaluators and evaluation participants to debates about the effectiveness of traditional evaluation methods in culturally diverse settings. The issue of inequity concerning the unequal playing field for evaluators of color was at the core of the situation that called for the GEDI program. Thus, the success of the GEDI program and its graduates cannot be disconnected from an examination of the ecosystem illustrated in Figure 7.1.

The organizations shown in Figure 7.1 have to be regarded as parts of a whole and dynamic system that can impact the role of evaluation in promoting equity, and not as independent and detached entities. If, for instance, funders require that evaluators consider the role of culture in affecting outcomes for communities of color and make this a part of their requests for proposals (including allowance for resources and time to support this), evaluation firms who respond to the request have to understand and practice culturally responsive evaluation. For funders to demonstrate this interest, AEA, as the national professional organization for evaluators, can support more debates and trainings about the practice of such evaluations.[1] As such, the competencies of GEDI program graduates will be valued and supported, and the field will become more ready for their participation.

There are specific actions that need to be considered to strengthen the ecosystem. These actions are borrowed from the literature about valuing and implementing diversity (see, e.g., Cross, Katz, Miller, & Seashore, 1994; Loden, 1996) and applied to the evaluation profession:

NEW DIRECTIONS FOR EVALUATION • DOI: 10.1002/ev

• Buy-in and involvement of influential leaders from AEA; the evaluation profession; the private, public, and nonprofit sectors that fund, conduct, or consume evaluations; and the academic sector that provides training and support to future social scientists and evaluators of color, to lift up the relationship between evaluation and equity.
• Review of institutional policies and practices that affect the recruitment, training, retention, and support of students and emerging professionals of color interested in evaluation.
• Further examination of the implicit biases and societal norms that affect perceptions of teachers, mentors, employers, and consumers who are integral to the training and support for evaluators of color.
• An independent or collective plan among key stakeholders (e.g., AEA and entities that fund and use evaluation) to address institutional policies and practices that limit the opportunities and resources available for evaluators of color and implicit biases toward evaluators of color.

Conclusion

The importance of understanding and targeting the ecosystem described in this chapter is underscored by existing literature about pipeline programs and their necessity. While there have been studies suggesting that institutional responses to professionals of color and practices aimed at promoting equity have improved due to concerted efforts by leaders in the profession and foundations (see, e.g., Johnson, 2012; Leviton, 2009; Patterson & Carline, 2006), there also have been studies that suggest that we have a long way to go in terms of affecting institutional policies and practices that exclude professionals of color and their work. For example, a recent study revealed disparities in the distribution of National Institutes of Health (NIH) research grants (Ginther et al., 2011). Even after controlling for training, previous grants, publications, and citations, study results showed that African American scholars received fewer grants than White scholars. Further, only 27% of bachelor's degrees earned by students of color between 2009 and 2010 (National Center for Education Statistics, 2012) and only 18% of non-Whites serve as college and university faculty (National Center for Education Statistics, 2011).

A review of the literature on diversity pipeline programs also revealed that most of the strategies are predominately focused on change at the individual level (Cantor, Bergeisen, & Baker, 1998; Grumbach et al., 2003; Tietjen-Smith, Davis, Williams, & Anderson, 2009). The GEDI program is no exception; the authors believe that this is partly due to the limited resources for the program to strategize, promote, and sustain the involvement of public and private funders, organizations that receive contracts to conduct evaluation, professional associations, and academic institutions. Yet, it is imperative for pipeline programs to move beyond the individual and consider the interconnected parts of the ecosystem (i.e., organizational policies and practices, institutional norms) that made it necessary for the programs in the first place and thus play a role in the change process (Collins & Hopson, 2007). Focusing on and affecting individuals—the student or intern, in particular—is less threatening than challenging policies and practices that have been in place for generations. Also, individual-level outcomes will take less time to observe compared to organizational- and system-level outcomes. Nevertheless, accounting for strategies and outcomes at the organization and profession levels—which means looking at the ecosystem in its entirety—is critical because underlying the goals and assumptions of diversity pipeline programs is the intent to promote equity for groups that have historically been excluded from certain resources and opportunities (Grantmakers in Health, 2001; Johnson, 2012; Lee & Nemes, 2010; Leviton, 2009). The results of these efforts will also increase the United States' ability to compete globally, which requires workers with technical knowledge and skills, as well as knowledge of other cultures and skills, to work across cultures (National Academy of Sciences, 2007).

Note

1. The development and dissemination of cultural competency by AEA was the first step in this direction.

References

Association for the Study and Development of Community (ASDC). (2000). *Building diversity initiative proposal.* Prepared for the W. K. Kellogg Foundation. Gaithersburg, MD: Author.

Association for the Study and Development of Community (ASDC). (2002) *Building diversity initiative plan.* Prepared for the W. K. Kellogg Foundation. Gaithersburg, MD: Author.

Cantor, J. C., Bergeisen, L., & Baker, L. (1998). Effect of an intensive educational program for minority college students and recent graduates on the probability of acceptance to medical school. *Journal of the American Medical Association, 280*(9), 772–776.

Collins, P., & Hopson, R. (2007). Building leadership development, social justice, and social change in evaluation through a pipeline program. In K. Hannum, J. Martineau, & C. Reinelt (Eds.), *Handbook of leadership development evaluation* (pp. 173–198). San Francisco, CA: Wiley.

Cross, E. Y., Katz, J. H., Miller, F. A., & Seashore, E. W. (Eds.). (1994). *The promise of diversity.* Burr Ridge, IL: IRWIN Professional Publishing.

Deaux, K., & Ullman, J. (1983). *Women of steel.* New York, NY: Praeger.

Ginther, D., Schaffer, W. T., Schnell, J., Masimore, B., Liu, F., Haak, L., & Kington, R. (2011). Race, ethnicity, and NIH awards. *Science, 33*, 1015–1019.

Grant, D., & Oswick, C. (2010). Actioning organizational discourse to re-articulate change practice. *Practising Social Change, 2*, 19–24.

Grantmakers in Health. (2001, November). *Promoting diversity in the health workforce.* Washington, DC: Author.

Grumbach, K., Coffman, J., Rosenoff, E., Muñoz, C., Gandara, P., & Sepulveda, E. (2003). *Strategies for improving the diversity of the health professions.* Retrieved from http://www.familymedicine.medschool.ucsf.edu/pdf/div_strategies.pdf

Hood, S. (2004). A journey to understand the role of culture in program evalua-
tion: Snapshots and personal reflections of one African American evaluator. In M.
Thompson-Robinson, R. Hopson, & S. SenGupta (Eds.), *New Direction for Evaluation:
No. 102. In search of cultural competence in evaluation: Toward principles and practices*
(pp. 21–37). San Francisco, CA: Jossey-Bass. doi:10.1002/ev.113
Johnson, E. C., Jr. (2012). Increasing diversity and creating responsible citizens and
leaders. *Michigan Bar Journal, 91*(1), 32–34.
Lee, K., & Nemes, M. (2010). *Final evaluation report for the diversifying leadership for
sustainable food policy initiative.* Gaithersburg, MD: Community Science.
Leviton, L. C. (2009). Foreword. *Journal of Dental Education, 73*(2), S5–S7.
Loden, M. (1996). *Implementing diversity.* New York, NY: McGraw-Hill.
National Academy of Sciences. (2007). *Rising above the gathering storm.* Washington,
DC: National Academies Press.
National Center for Education Statistics. (2011). *Integrated postsecondary education data
system [data system].* Retrieved from http://nces.ed.gov/ipeds/
National Center for Education Statistics. (2012). *The condition of education 2012
(NCES Publication No. 2012045).* Retrieved from http://nces.ed.gov/pubsearch
/pubsinfo.asp?pubid=2012045
Patterson, D. G., & Carline, J. D. (2006). Promoting minority access to health careers
through health profession-public school partnerships: A review of the literature. *Academic Medicine, 81*(6), S5–S10.
SenGupta, S., Hopson, R., & Thompson-Robinson, M. (2004). Cultural competence
in evaluation: An overview. In M. Thompson-Robinson, R. Hopson, & S. SenGupta
(Eds.), *New Direction for Evaluation: No. 102. In search of cultural competence in evaluation: Toward principles and practices* (pp. 5–19). San Francisco, CA: Jossey-Bass.
doi:10/1002/ev.112
Symonette, H. (2004). Walking pathways toward becoming a culturally competent evaluator: Boundaries, borderlands, and crossings. In M. Thompson-Robinson, R. Hopson, & S. SenGupta (Eds.), *New Direction for Evaluation: No. 102. In search of cultural
competence in evaluation: Toward principles and practices* (pp. 95–109). San Francisco,
CA: Jossey-Bass. doi:10.1002/ev.118
Thomas, V., & Stevens, F. (Eds.). (2004). *New Directions for Evaluation: No. 101. Co-
constructing a contextually responsive evaluation framework: The talent development
model of school reform.* San Francisco, CA: Jossey-Bass.
Thompson-Robinson, M., Hopson, R., & SenGupta, S. (Eds.). (2004). *New Directions
for Evaluation: No. 102. In search of cultural competence in evaluation: Toward principles
and practices.* San Francisco, CA: Jossey-Bass.
Tietjen-Smith, T., Davis, C., Williams, A., & Anderson, G. (2009). A national study of
baccalaureate degree completions in the sciences: An overview of institutional success
by public, private, and proprietary. *Academic Leadership, 7.* Retrieved from http://www
.academicleadership.org
Toren, N., & Kraus, V. (1987). The effects of minority size on women's position in
academia. *Social Forces, 65,* 1090–1100.

KIEN LEE *is the vice president and principal associate at Community Science,
Gaithersburg, MD, where she has worked with several GEDI program graduates who were employed by Community Science. She worked on the Building
Diversity Initiative, which led to the creation of the GEDI program and was
also involved as a mentor and presenter for the first five cohorts of interns.*

BRANDI GILBERT *is an associate at Community Science, Gaithersburg, MD, and
former GEDI intern in the fifth cohort, Legacy.*

8

How Will We Know It When We See It? A Critical Friend Perspective of the Graduate Education Diversity Internship (GEDI) Program and Its Legacy in Evaluation

Stafford Hood

Abstract

As a critical friend of the Graduate Education Diversity Internship (GEDI) program, I provide three personal reference points to organize observations and reflections during my role as mentor and instructor for the program. As a scholar concerned with promoting Culturally Responsive Evaluation (CRE), I reflect on the founding and development of the program alongside some of the key ideas that shaped CRE with the hopeful assumptions that the GEDI alumni will carry the CRE torch that lights the path for those who will follow in this common struggle. © Wiley Periodicals, Inc., and the American Evaluation Association.

I t has been a personal challenge to capture, prioritize, and then think about how I would articulate in writing my many reflections about the Graduate Education Diversity Internship (GEDI) program since its inception and what we know it to be today. The reference points for these reflections are primarily based on my membership on the AEA Advisory Oversight Committee of the Building Diversity Initiative (2001), member of the AEA Diversity Committee (Chair 2001), presenter/mentor for several

NEW DIRECTIONS FOR EVALUATION, no. 143, Fall 2014   © 2014 Wiley Periodicals, Inc., and the American Evaluation
Association.   Published online in Wiley Online Library (wileyonlinelibrary.com) • DOI: 10.1002/ev.20097

of the GEDI cohorts (2004–2008), and just simply what might be characterized as one of the "uncles" in the GEDI extended family. At the same time, these reference points are also interconnected and ran parallel to the work I was undertaking individually and with others during the birth and evolution of the GEDI program.

Based on my early conversations about this *New Directions for Evaluation* (NDE) issue, *Building a New Generation of Culturally Responsive Evaluators Through AEA's Graduate Education Diversity Internship Program,* the initial plan was for me to reflect on "the potential legacy of the GEDI program for AEA and the field of evaluation in general." If that was not enough, there was also the suggestion (from someone—maybe myself) that I would in some way "imagine" what might be the potential contribution/impact that this and other kindred programs could/should make over the next 10 years. For example, should we expect these programs to produce a cadre of evaluators who would explore, inform, and/or generate important global discoveries and innovations in the field of evaluation? Some of us would hope that the cadre of young evaluators that have been and will be trained through the GEDI program will continue the change we envision from this movement. In fact, those who have been the beneficiaries of similar training experiences in graduate degree and nondegree training programs (with a core culturally responsive evaluation orientation) can be viewed as "kindred cousins" of the GEDI. While there are probably numerous examples, I believe that kindred cousins have been produced in the graduate degree programs at Arizona State University, Duquesne University, and the University of Illinois at Urbana-Champaign and nondegree programs such as the Howard University Evaluation Training Institute and Robert Wood Johnson Foundation Evaluation Fellow program over the past decade. It is their time, but we cannot expect them to fight this battle without our continued counsel and support. We must continually remind ourselves what Malcom X knew to be true about college students in 1964 (and in our case graduate students or young CRE evaluators) when he stated:

> The students all over the world are the ones who bring about change; old people don't bring about change. I mean I'm not saying this against anybody that's old because if you're ready for some action you're not old. As long as you want some action you're young. But any time you begin to sit on the fence, and your toes start shaking because you're afraid too much action is going down, then you're too old. (Malcom X, Homecoming Rally of the OAAHU August 29, 1964, cited in Breitman, 1970, p. 143)

I definitely do not see myself as being too old to continue as an active participant of this movement nor believe this is the case for others in my "graying" cohort of peers.

It is not likely that what I have written in these few pages can or should fully address what has been or can be the legacy of this evaluation internship program or our responsibility as the uncles and aunts in this common struggle. However, within this conversation are some of the right questions we must challenge ourselves to address. The thoughts and ruminations written here will be attentive to the initial conceptualization of this "critical friend perspective," but they are primarily intended for the GEDI, future GEDI, their kindred cadre of young non-GEDI evaluators, and those of us who see ourselves as GEDI uncles and aunts.

It has been instructive for me to reflect on my participation, my projects, my writings, and other related experiences that were inextricably connected to the fundamental purpose and conceptualization of the GEDI program. This program and other related efforts has been a collective mission to understand and advocate for the relevance of culture and cultural context in evaluation theory and practice or what some of us call "culturally responsive evaluation" (CRE). There is indeed a symbiotic relationship between CRE and the critical importance of a dramatic increase in the pool of highly trained evaluators of color and others who are grounded in the centrality of culture and cultural context in evaluation. As I went through the mental process to organize my thoughts to write this "critical friend" reflection, three personal reference points were the most prominent. The first is the five years preceding the first AEA/Duquesne Internship cohort of 2004, which I would characterize as a period of heightening the awareness of CRE and the need for a more racially diverse evaluation community. The second personal reference point is my involvement and interactions with several cohorts of GEDI interns through their development as evaluators from early childhood, adolescence, and young adulthood. My third reference point was my experience in codirecting an evaluation project with Rodney Hopson and seeing the post internship talents on display in the evaluation of the North Carolina Alliance to Create Opportunity through Education in 2011.

Reflective Reference Point 1: Heightening the Importance of Culturally Responsive Evaluation and the Need for More Evaluators of Color

My first reference point for this reflection was the period of 1998 through 2003. Prior to 1998, my work had primarily focused on "culturally responsive assessment" (Hood, 1999a, 1999b); the limited production of minority doctoral recipients by top-ranked colleges and schools of education (Hood & Freeman 1995a); and the virtual absence of minority doctoral recipients in research methods, educational measurement, and statistics (Hood & Freeman, 1995b). My use of the term *culturally responsive assessment* was a direct result of this collaboration between key African American educational researchers who were (and continue to be) leading the investigation into the use of culturally responsive pedagogy (Gloria Ladson-Billings, University of Wisconsin-Madison and Carole Lee, Northwestern University) and those of us who were having a similar conversation about the reasonableness of developing culturally responsive/specific assessment approaches (Gwyneth Boodoo, ETS, Audrey Qualls, Iowa Testing Programs/University of Iowa, and myself). At that time I argued that the potential of culturally responsive pedagogy to be a more effective approach for teaching students of color,

> ... forces one to seriously consider the merits of developing assessment approaches that incorporate the basic tenets of culturally responsive pedagogical strategies, and that are grounded in the cultural context of diverse groups of examinees. Alternatively, it suggests that the student learning that results from culturally responsive instructional strategies may be more effectively assessed by using approaches that are also culturally responsive. (Hood, 1999b, p. 188)

Therefore, it is not surprising that the context of my thinking about culturally responsive assessment in 1998 also informed and influenced my ideas about CRE as I wrote the *Amistad* paper for the Robert Stake symposium at the University of Illinois at Urbana-Champaign (Hood, 1998). Even though I had been a practicing evaluator for nearly 15 years by 1998, I had only engaged in one substantive scholarly writing endeavor on evaluation (Hood & Frierson, 1994) until presenting the paper entitled *Responsive Evaluation Amistad Style: Perspectives of One African American Program Evaluator* at Robert Stake's retirement symposium in May 1998. Briefly, the *Amistad* case involved the case of 53 Africans of the Mende tribe who had been kidnapped from Sierra Leone mutinied aboard a Portuguese slave ship in 1939, killing all but two of their captors. The local abolitionists hired lawyer Roger Sherman Baldwin to defend the Mende, and he was later joined by John Quincy Adams (the sixth U.S. President, 1825–1829). The initial charges of murder and mutiny were dropped by a lower U.S. Court. However, the legal question for the U.S. Appellate and Supreme Courts was whether the Mende were property to be returned to Spain even though the slave trade had been outlawed by Spain, the U.S. government, and Britain. My example of the *Amistad* case made the point about how the absence of African or African Americans to participate in legal defense of the Mende was detrimental to them, as it is also the case when such an absence exists in evaluations conducted in communities of color.

One of the major challenges in providing an effective defense for the Mende was the language barrier between the defendants and their legal team as well as the cultural differences. In order to present an adequate and compelling argument, the defense team and the court needed to "understand" the Mende defendants' story of the incident. After several failed attempts that included a White Harvard linguist, an old local African who spoke the "Congo language," and two freed slaves from a British ship, with one being Mende. James Covey (the name he assumed) had been raised as Mende before being captured to be a slave but later freed by the British naval ship and taught to read and write English. Covey's lived experience as a Mende made him eminently qualified to serve as an interpreter and cultural liaison.

Inspired (maybe provoked) by the movie "Amistad," my paper at the Stake symposium argued that: (a) Stake's responsive evaluation approach provided a beginning framework for "culturally responsive evaluation," (b) the absence of African and/or African American professionals to assist in the legal defense of the Amistad Africans could be equated to the limited number of trained evaluators of color, and (c) an evaluator with a "lived experience" who could interpret and understand cultural values in evaluations undertaken in racially diverse communities was a necessity (Hood, 1998).

The year following the Stake Symposium, I cofounded Arizona State University's annual national conference on the Relevance of Assessment and Culture in Evaluation (RACE) with its inaugural conference in January 2000. Later that same year, I became a member of the AEA Building Diversity Initiative Advisory Oversight Committee and AEA Diversity Committee (Chair 2001). The interface between the RACE conference and AEA Building Diversity Initiative provided an "expanded space" for the conversations among researchers, scholars, and practitioners about the role of culture and cultural context in evaluation and assessment as well as the need to increase the number of trained evaluators and assessment specialists of color. This climate and heightened discourse contributed to the creation of the *Relevance of Culture in Evaluation Project* (RCEP) at Arizona State University that would be funded over a period of seven years with the support of four grants from the National Science Foundation.

The first phase of the RCEP was the *Relevance of Culture in Evaluation Workshops* (RCEW) I and II, which were held in January 2002 and January 2003, respectively, as preconference workshops of the annual RACE conference. The RCEWs focused on building the evaluation capacity of schools with high concentrations of racial minority and poor students by providing a group of teachers from these schools with a basic knowledge and understanding of educational evaluation. The next phase of the RCEP was designed and implemented with Co-PI Melvin Hall (Northern Arizona University) and funded by NSF in 2003 as the *Relevance of Culture in Evaluation Institute* (RCEI). RCEI established and trained school-based evaluation teams to conduct evaluations *responsive* to their schools' culture.

The RCEI also reflected a major linkage to AEA in general, but more significantly to the Building Diversity Initiative through its advisory board that included Jennifer Greene, Rodney Hopson, Karen Kirkhart, Joan LaFrance, and Hazel Symonette. The collective scholarly contributions and expertise in evaluation represented by the RCEI advisory board made a major contribution to the success of the project and the lessons learned. At the same time, the members of the RCEI advisory board's unwavering commitment to the importance of culture and cultural context in evaluation,

NEW DIRECTIONS FOR EVALUATION • DOI: 10.1002/ev

combined with their commitment to increase the diversity of the evaluation community, was an important asset not only to the project but also to
the work that would emanate in the future.

One of the first significant contributions of the RCEI advisory board
was the articulation of a vision that would guide our work on the project.
It was affectionately titled the RCEI "manifesto" as our definition of
evaluation:

> We Believe that evaluation is a learned practice that generates claims to know
> and claims of value, intended to be useful for informing policy and organi-
> zational decisions, learning about persistent social problems and how best
> to address them, improving existing social programs, or advancing ideas of
> equity, fairness and justice. (Hood et al., 2004)

Similarly, RCEI believed that the culturally responsive evaluator:

- must prioritize and be responsive to the needs and cultural parameters of
  those who are being served relative to the implementation of a program
  and its outcomes;
- involves self in learning, engaging, and appreciating the role of culture(s)
  within the context of the evaluation; and
- learns to recognize dissonance within the evaluation context, for example, between school and community group being served (Hood et al.,
  2004).

The RCEI manifesto and what we believed to be the profile of an aspiring culturally responsive evaluator guided the training and technical assistance that were provided to the participating RCEI school-based evaluation
teams. Each of the school-based teams faced considerable challenges during
their projects, but ultimately they successfully designed and implemented
CRE strategies.

While the RCEI successfully established school-based evaluation teams
in four elementary schools in the Phoenix metropolitan area with majority racial minority and poor students as well as one Navajo Nation elementary school (initially two), there was an additional yet not strategically
planned significant outcome. This outcome was the notable development of
the multiethnic group of seven Arizona State University doctoral students
who worked as research assistants on both the RCEW and RCEI projects.
These students received substantive training in CRE theory and practice as
a result of graduate courses in evaluation at ASU, extensive participation in
all phases of the RCEP, and the mentoring they received from all members
of the RCEI advisory board.

The Relevance of Culture in Evaluation Project provided an initial
space to expand and explore in more depth CRE from a theoretical orientation as well as related strategies for evaluation practice. This orientation and

the related strategies were translated by the RCEP into profession development training and technical assistance to build CRE capacity in low-income schools that served predominantly racial minority students. An unplanned outcome was the academic knowledge, training, and mentoring received by the six ASU doctoral students who served as research assistants on the RCEP and developed relationships as "cousins" to the first GEDI cohort in 2004. Therefore, this first reference point illustrates that the movement to increase CRE strategies and increase the presence of evaluators of color (with the GEDI program being one vehicle to accomplish this) did not happen in isolation of other efforts being undertaken by an emerging community of evaluators who were and were not a part of the BDI.

Reference Point 2: Early Childhood, Adolescence, and Young Adulthood of the Internship Program

In some ways, as I became a bit more conscious about the growth, training, and mentoring experiences of the ASU/RCEP doctoral students, I may have also been a bit more prepared for my involvement with the first AEA/Duquesne University Internship cohort in 2004. By chance, the RCEP doctoral students attended the same AEA annual conference as the first AEA/Duquesne Interns, and they established an immediate connection and sense of community. In many ways, they shared similar core readings, training experiences, and mentors within the CRE community and were "cousins."

Over the years, I have been a participant-observer in the developmental stages of the internship program from early childhood, adolescence, and where I think the program may be now in a period of young adulthood. My association has spanned this continuum at different times with different cohorts. Like many of the members of the BDI committee and RCEI advisory board, I have played a number of roles by providing workshops, reviewing applications for the program, mentoring individual interns, and participating in various roles at graduation sessions. It is apparent to me that since the start of this millennium a community of culturally diverse evaluation theorist, scholars, and practitioners has grown out of BDI, ASU/RCEP, and now GEDI. In fact this community is also a global one. In fact the GEDI environment was another "space" that facilitated the building of this community as we were brought together as a community/family of uncles, aunts, nieces, and nephews to share and learn from each other. It was often the case (appropriately so) that the roles of teacher and student were interchangeable. There have indeed been expansions, refinements, and evolution of the internship program over the years. Different coordinators, visions, approaches, and groups of interns have (predictably) produced different individual and collective experiences. However, there appears to be three constants associated with the internship program: the quality of the

NEW DIRECTIONS FOR EVALUATION • DOI: 10.1002/ev

interns, the sense of community they built among themselves, and sustaining this sense of community after completion of the program.

Over the years, it has always brought a smile to my face and warmth to my heart when I found myself in the GEDI environment. Seeing the faces of old and new GEDI reminded me that it had not been long ago that the visible presence of this growing critical mass of young racially diverse, socially responsible, and culturally responsive grounded evaluators was not evident in our evaluation community. They were our dream waiting to be manifested if we continued to be agitators for this cause and persevered. I observed the different cohorts of interns begin their respective internship programs, move through various phases of the curriculum and training experiences, and then visibly be transformed before our eyes in their knowledge, skills, passion, and confidence they displayed as aspiring culturally responsive evaluators, each in their own way. I reflected on this transformation, their responsibilities, and challenges out loud at the 2008 graduation of the fourth cohort when I stated:

> If you listen closely, you may also hear the voices and footsteps of those who will follow you, those who you will train and those who you will mentor to do the important work that is ahead. You will certainly face challenges in your continuing development as an evaluator and hopefully a socially responsible one committed to social justice in your respective disciplines. You should expect no less because this is how it has been and should be if you truly want to make a difference in the lives of those who have not been as privileged as we have been. (Hood, 2008)

I believed then as I do now that as evaluators we must be the "agitators" Frederick Douglass called for in (1857) and the "liberators" called for by Asa Hilliard III (2000) when we work within and across our culturally diverse communities. I also believe that Hilliard provided a set of criteria for what should be expected of culturally responsive evaluators: Culturally responsive evaluators are those who:

- "are rooted in a deep understanding of our [the group's] culture and traditions,
- identify with and are a part of us . . . [and] . . .
- see our children as their own." (Hilliard, 2000, p. 14)

From my admittedly biased perspective I still believe that the GEDI should resonate and act upon the principles of Douglass and Hilliard in their journey as evaluators. Therefore, no one would be surprised that these are the principles that are at the core of how I have engaged the GEDI experience as a presenter and/or mentor. Of course, this will also be true for any future involvement I will have with the program if invited.

Reference Point 3: The Post Internship Talents on Display in the Evaluation of the North Carolina Alliance to Create Opportunity Through Education

My third reference point in providing this critical friend perspective was my experience in codirecting an evaluation project with Rodney Hopson as a member of the Culturally Responsive Evaluation Collaboration (CREC) evaluation team. Probably one of the most important indicators of how the GEDI program impacted the development of the interns is ultimately how they engaged their craft as contributing members of the evaluation community and particularly the CRE community as university faculty, scholars, and/or practitioners. Watching firsthand the GEDI evaluation interns bring their knowledge, skills, and grounding in CRE to an evaluation project provides (at least in my mind) one of the most important examples of the program's impact on the participants.

During the period of July 2011 to October 2012, Rodney Hopson and I codirected an evaluation of the North Carolina Alliance to Create Opportunity through Education collaboration by our CREC evaluation team. In addition to Rodney Hopson and me, the evaluation team was comprised of two alumni of the GEDI program and two GEDI "cousins." Wanda Casillas and Ricardo Gomez were members of the last AEA/Duquesne Evaluation Internship program directed by Rodney Hopson in 2008–2009. One of the cousins (Summer Jackson) was an alumnus of the Robert Wood Johnson Evaluation Fellowship program (codirected by Rodney Hopson), and the other cousin (Khawla Obeidat) had been one of the ASU/RCEP doctoral students from 2003 to 2007. At the time we conducted this evaluation, Khawla was an assistant professor of educational psychology at University of Colorado at Denver; Wanda Casillas and Ricardo Gomez were completing their doctoral dissertations at Cornell University and University of Massachusetts-Amherst, respectively; and Summer Jackson was an independent consultant and administrator for the Bay Area Blacks in Philanthropy and senior research assistant for Davis Ja & Associates.

The evaluation of the North Carolina Alliance to Create Opportunity through Education was undertaken to evaluate the "effectiveness of the *North Carolina Alliances for Graduate Education and the Professoriate (AGEP)* program in achieving its stated objectives [and] focused on NC AGEPs programming activities, experiences of participants (current students and alumni) and experiences of institutions/programs as members of the *North Carolina Alliance to Create Opportunity through Education (OPT-ED)*" (CREC, 2012, p. 9). The evaluation of this alliance was an ideal opportunity for the evaluation team to apply its specialized talents and experiences in CRE to a project that had been designed and implemented to "increase the presence and persistence of underrepresented minorities in STEM fields" (CREC, 2012, p. 9). Each member of the CREC team brought their unique knowledge, skills, and experiences in evaluation to the project with strong quantitative, qualitative, and mixed methods skills represented in different degrees across the members of the team. At the same time, the orientation and grounding in CRE was at the core of each member's orientation to the project and practice. This was reflected at each phase of the evaluation from the development of the evaluation design, development of instruments (surveys and interview protocols), implementation, analysis, and development of the final report.

As I reflect on this experience, what stands out about our younger members of the team was the level of excellence they exhibited in their respective knowledge and skill sets combined with their work ethic and confidence as contributing members of the team. There were indeed times when our (Hopson and my) lead senior evaluation responsibilities took precedence over this particular evaluation project, but the other members of the team were able to effectively make progress on the tasks that needed to be accomplished assuming responsibilities among themselves. Knowing how well each of them had been trained and who had "touched" them in this training, I had a sense of comfortable confidence. At the same time, the project also provided us senior evaluators with an extensive amount of time for close interaction, more teaching, and more mentoring that would hopefully contribute to their further development as evaluators in general and culturally responsive evaluators in particular.

Summarizing the Reflections of This Critical Friend and Ponderings About the Future

The need to increase the number of culturally responsive evaluators globally continues to be critically important as racial and cultural demographics continue to rapidly change in countries that had been historically more homogeneous (i.e., Ireland, Netherlands, …). As an evaluation community we all face similar current, historical, and future challenges regarding the extent to which evaluation can/will/should contribute in efforts to improve the educational, social, political, and economic circumstances of the traditionally disenfranchised in our respective global and national societies.

The necessity for evaluation efforts to address the needs of the traditionally disenfranchised in the global context must never be ignored or underemphasized. Consequently, I remain firm in my belief and conviction that as evaluators we must continue to increase our understanding, develop, and refine evaluation strategies so that they are more culturally responsive. I believe that the GEDI evaluation internship program has the potential to serve as a model that could accomplish this goal, and a closer evaluation of it is certainly necessary. In fact some of the work presented in this NDE may have provided steps in that direction.

The three references points that guided my reflections have told three separate but interrelated stories. The first reference point of *heightening the awareness of culturally responsive evaluation and the need for a more racially diverse evaluation community* provided at least partial illumination about the period immediately prior to the birth of the first cohort of interns in 2004. Unquestionably the birth of this internship program must be rightfully credited to the core AEA BDI leadership during its formative years (Symonette, Mertens, & Hopson, Chapter 1 of this issue). Their unwavering effort and tireless commitment are responsible for us being able to have this discussion today. However, my first reference point shows that movement to increase CRE strategies and presence of racial minorities in the evaluation community with the GEDI program being one vehicle to accomplish this did not happen in isolation of other efforts being undertaken by an emerging community of evaluators who were and were not a part of the BDI. The period that birthed the AEA internship program inextricably connected to the rapidly increasing discourse about the critical importance of culture and cultural context in evaluation that also required an increase in the presence of racial minorities in the evaluation community.

The second reference point provided reflections as a participant observer of the internship program (in varying degrees across cohorts) as it moved through its stages *from early childhood, adolescence, and what I believe is its current period of young adulthood.* Based on my observations and interactions with the internship program since 2004, and admittedly with some limitations to the overall knowledge I possess about the total program, I identified what I believe are two major strengths of the program. The first obvious strength is that the quality of each intern individually and collectively in their respective cohorts has been outstanding. Of course, starting with a good product typically will yield outstanding results, but it was particularly evident at the end of the internship program that the individual interns and their respective cohorts had been "transformed" in their growth as evaluators as well as their confidence and commitment to making a difference. However, I am not certain about the extent that each intern and cohort were genuinely committed to becoming a culturally responsive evaluator or if that was always clearly a priority that was embedded in their internship experience. The debate about culture and cultural context in evaluation continues as well as our refinement of how CRE should be defined. The question "How do we know CRE when we see it?" is both a practical and an empirical question that must be closely examined during the pre- and post-GEDI internship experience. Thus far it does not appear that this has been one of the core questions across the GEDI cohorts, of course unless I missed it.

A second obvious strength of the program is the sense of community that was evident for each cohort of interns. This could be an invaluable asset as they move through their professional careers to have a supportive network that can serve both professional and personal development needs. The question is: to what extent is this sense of community evident across other internship cohorts and whether it is extended to their GEDI cousins with similar training, experiences, and commitment? As I have observed several

GEDI cohorts both near and far, it is obvious that the sense of community among the interns and directors develops over time and is strengthened across cohorts. It is reasonable to suggest that the longevity of GEDI directors leading the program is most likely to more effectively build a sense of community but we may also want to examine how long it takes for this to happen. Of course the question is also whether this should be a priority? I think it should be.

My final reference point reflection was based on my experience in codirecting the evaluation project with Rodney Hopson as I saw firsthand the post internship talents on display in the evaluation of the North Carolina Alliance to Create Opportunity through Education. In this case, I made the point that as members of our evaluation team each of our younger members met and often exceeded my expectations in the multiple skills, work ethic, and grounding in CRE they displayed as evaluators. In fact I can honestly say that each of them exhibited knowledge and skills that I would have expected from much more experienced evaluators. In my mind, this is one of the most credible pieces of evidence about the outcomes of this evaluation internship model and/or the same type of training and experiences that can occur within a graduate degree program.

So I guess one could surmise from my comments that my reflections have been generally positive about the internship program and the interns who have completed the program. However, my writing this critical friend's reflection has forced me to have other conversations with my more senior peers of GEDI uncles and aunts about the extent to which we have met our responsibilities to the interns after they have completed the program. While I know it is true that all of us GEDI uncles and aunts have in some way continued to serve as mentors to some of them and have provided a range of and degrees of professional development and personal support to GEDI until this day. What I find to be lacking is that we have not thought in any systematic way about the type of intellectual and professional development support we should provide during the *post*-internship phase of their development as culturally responsive evaluators, if that is the path they have chosen.

I do not think it is unreasonable for us to expect that at least some interns/students/trainees will become active members of our community. As the more senior members of this community, we should also be informed by their experiences, learning from what they identify as strengths and weaknesses of the approaches that have been used. We should also expect them to teach others about their internship/training experiences, while seeking ways to improve the learning experiences of the cadre of culturally responsive evaluators to follow them.

Each of the interns will pursue their respective careers as university faculty, university administrators, researchers, practicing evaluators, managers, etc. Should we not also have some responsibility for helping them to successfully navigate the still treacherous waters before them in this journey? Should we not have a plan for how we might be "responsive" to their new set of needs for their new challenges? I currently do not have an answer to these questions, but I think they are some of the right questions.

References

Breitman, G. (Ed.). (1970). *By any means necessary: Speeches, interviews and a letter by Malcolm X.* New York, NY: Pathfinder Press.
Culturally Responsive Evaluation Collaboration (CREC). (2012, November). *Final evaluation report.* North Carolina Alliance to Create Opportunity through Education.
Hilliard, A. G. (2000, April). *The state of African education.* Paper presented at the annual meeting of the American Educational Research Association, New Orleans, LA.
Hood, S. (1998). Responsive evaluation Amistad style: Perspectives of one African American program evaluator. In R. Davis (Ed.), *Proceedings of the Robert E. Stake symposium on educational evaluation* (pp. 101–112). Urbana-Champaign: University of Illinois.
Hood, S. (1999a). Assessment in the context of culture and pedagogy: A collaborative effort, a meaningful goal. *The Journal of Negro Education, 67*(3), 184–186.
Hood, S. (1999b). Culturally responsive performance-based assessment: Conceptual and psychometric considerations. *The Journal of Negro Education, 67*(3), 187–197.
Hood, S. (2008, November). *American Evaluation Association/Duquesne University internship commencement address.* Paper presented at the annual meeting of the American Evaluation Association, Denver, CO.
Hood, S., & Freeman, D. (1995a). Where do students of color earn doctorates in education?: The "Top 25" colleges and schools of education. *Journal of Negro Education, 64*(4), 423–436.
Hood, S., & Freeman, D. (1995b, April). *Breaking the tradition: Increasing the production of doctoral recipients of color in research methods, educational measurement, and statistics.* Paper presented at the annual meeting of the American Educational Research Association, San Francisco, CA.
Hood, S., & Frierson, H., Jr. (Eds.). (1994). *Beyond the dream: Meaningful program evaluation and assessment to achieve equal opportunity at predominantly White universities.* Greenwich, CN: JAI Press.
Hood, S., Hall, M., Kirkhart, K. E., Hopson, R. K., Greene, J. C., LaFrance, J., & Symonette, H. (2004). *Relevance of culture in evaluation institute: A manifesto.* Unpublished manuscript, Directorate for Education and Human Resources, Division of Research, Evaluation, and Communications, National Science Foundation, Arlington, VA.

STAFFORD HOOD is Sheila M. Miller Professor and the associate dean for research and research education and director of the Center for Culturally Responsive Evaluation and Assessment, College of Education, University of Illinois at Urbana-Champaign. He served as an advisor, instructor, and mentor for the GEDI program as well as a member of the AEA Building Diversity Initiative Advisory Oversight Committee and AEA Diversity Committee (Chair 2001).

INDEX

NEW DIRECTIONS FOR EVALUATION

ORDER FORM SUBSCRIPTION AND SINGLE ISSUES

DISCOUNTED BACK ISSUES:

Use this form to receive 20% off all back issues of *New Directions for Evaluation*.
All single issues priced at **$23.20** (normally $29.00)

TITLE	ISSUE NO.	ISBN

*Call 888-378-2537 or see mailing instructions below. When calling, mention the promotional code JBNND
to receive your discount. For a complete list of issues, please visit www.josseybass.com/go/ev*

SUBSCRIPTIONS: (1 YEAR, 4 ISSUES)

☐ New Order ☐ Renewal

U.S.	☐ Individual: $89	☐ Institutional: $334
CANADA/MEXICO	☐ Individual: $89	☐ Institutional: $374
ALL OTHERS	☐ Individual: $113	☐ Institutional: $408

*Call 888-378-2537 or see mailing and pricing instructions below.
Online subscriptions are available at www.onlinelibrary.wiley.com*

ORDER TOTALS:

Issue / Subscription Amount: $ _____

Shipping Amount: $ _____
(for single issues only – subscription prices include shipping)

Total Amount: $ _____

SHIPPING CHARGES:

First Item	$6.00
Each Add'l Item	$2.00

*(No sales tax for U.S. subscriptions. Canadian residents, add GST for subscription orders. Individual rate subscriptions must
be paid by personal check or credit card. Individual rate subscriptions may not be resold as library copies.)*

BILLING & SHIPPING INFORMATION:

☐ **PAYMENT ENCLOSED:** *(U.S. check or money order only. All payments must be in U.S. dollars.)*

☐ **CREDIT CARD:** ☐ VISA ☐ MC ☐ AMEX

Card number _____Exp. Date_____

Card Holder Name_____Card Issue # _____

Signature _____Day Phone _____

☐ **BILL ME:** *(U.S. institutional orders only. Purchase order required.)*

Purchase order #_____
Federal Tax ID 13559302 • GST 89102-8052

Name _____

Address_____

Phone_____ E-mail_____

Copy or detach page and send to: **John Wiley & Sons, One Montgomery Street, Suite 1200,
San Francisco, CA 94104-4594**

Order Form can also be faxed to: **888-481-2665**

PROMO JBNND